Lotus Elan and Europa

Lotus Elan and Europa

A collector's guide
by John Bolster

MOTOR RACING PUBLICATIONS LTD
Unit 6, The Pilton Estate, 46 Pitlake, Croydon CR0 3RA, England

First published 1980
Reprinted 1981
Reprinted 1985
Reprinted 1992
ISBN 0-900549-48-3

Printed in Great Britain by The Amadeus Press Limited,
Huddersfield, West Yorkshire

Contents

Introduction

This is a book about the second phase of Lotus history. The first phase was that of the do-it-yourself cars, generally competition-orientated; the third and current phase has seen the Lotus become an up-market super car. For many enthusiasts, the middle period is the most rewarding because the cars are so collectable.

Some of the great cars of the recent past are quite unsuitable for the amateur collector. They are of a size and complexity that place their repair and reconditioning beyond the capacity of a modest home workshop. A complete rebuild would compel the unfortunate owner to call constantly on the services of specialist firms, with the inevitable result that he would run out of money with the job half completed.

The Lotus models covered by this book are of brilliantly original design, but many of their components have been adapted from more mundane vehicles, which assists enormously in the acquisition of cheap spare parts. Although these types no longer figure in the Lotus catalogue, arrangements have been made for the future manufacture of such essential items as chassis frames, while the servicing of the twin-cam engine is assured.

Above all, these cars are marvellous fun to drive, and the jaded motorist, who has become bored with his everyday journeys, can recapture the thrill of driving for pleasure. Though it's vulgar to talk about money, it might be whispered that the Lotus models with which we are here concerned are all appreciating investments, so one could enjoy one's hobby and finish up with a profit, which is a somewhat rare achievement.

When preparing this opus, it has been a refreshing experience to become involved in the tremendous enthusiasm that surrounds the marque, Lotus. I would like to take this opportunity of thanking all those who helped me to write this book, and particularly: my wife, for much hard work and encouragement and for keeping up the alcohol level in my blood stream.

My friends at Lotus, who supplied me with abundant information and documentation, especially Donovan McLauchlan, Roy Badcock and Dennis Jewell.

Jabby Crombac, *pour son article si sympathique.*

Ian Webb, Bobby Bell and Martin Colvill, who arranged for me to drive the cars and provided me with much valuable Lotus lore.

Nick Atkins, who taught me all the secrets of the Lotus 47.

John Miles and Graham Warner, for details of their racing successes.

Doug Nye and Ian H. Smith, the authors of two excellent books on Lotus that gave me much background knowledge.

November 1979   JOHN BOLSTER

The Mark 6 was the first true Lotus production car, and like its hand-built predecessors it was competition-bred. Most were assembled from a kit of components, and specifications varied considerably. Here, an example with de Dion rear suspension and optional wire wheels is locked in close combat with a live-axle example with standard wheels. Engines varied from 1172 cc side-valve Ford to 2-litre BMW.

CHAPTER 1

Ancestors and parentage

From Austin Seven to Elite

This is not the place nor have we the space, to write a history of Lotus. Indeed, the single-seaters, with which the *marque* is so deeply involved, have little to do with this particular story. Nevertheless, it is necessary to go back to the beginning, if only to understand why such a bewildering variety of cars have carried the Lotus name.

For example, every Lotus did not emerge from the gates of that beautiful factory at Hethel, in Norfolk. Mark 1 was originally designed by Sir Herbert Austin, on his billiard table it is said, but in 1948 it was redesigned as a Lotus trials car by a young university student named Colin Chapman. Like many of the finest specials, it was built in a lockup garage to the dismay of the neighbours, and so was Mark 2, which combined the best parts of Sir Herbert's famous Seven with Henry Ford's 1172 cc power unit, its constructor by then being in the RAF.

Mark 3 went back to an Austin engine, in order to compete in the races organized by the 750 Club. Actually, it didn't compete, it just walked all over the other competitors, so great was its superiority. Even thus early, in 1951, this car showed that Chapman knew exactly what he was doing. Other 750 racers had hard springs and whippy chassis, but the Lotus was softly sprung and the frame was braced by a triangulated tubular erection over the engine, as well as being welded into a box section throughout its length. Independent front suspension on the swing-axle principle was achieved by splitting a Ford axle, chosen because it had bigger brakes than those of the Austin Seven.

Now we come to a most important point in the story, for Colin Chapman acquired the first Lotus factory. It was a stable in Tottenham Lane, Hornsey, and on January 1, 1952, the Lotus Engineering Company was registered. Actually, the Managing Director was employed by the British Oxygen Company, then and for a while afterwards, and he only became a car manufacturer in the evenings and at weekends. The first product was Mark 4, ordered by Mike Lawson, who had previously bought Mark 2; it was a trials and autocross car that could also be used on the road.

Mark 4 was another happy marriage of Austin and Ford, but with many Lotus touches about it, and Lawson won a whole string of events, even against specials that arrived on trailers. Mark 5 was to have been the Austin Seven to end Austin Sevens, but it was never completed because a new project became such a success.

This was Mark 6, which was based on a multi-tubular spaceframe with stressed aluminium floor and body panels. If you have an open car with a spaceframe, you cannot cut holes in the sides for doors, but who wants doors, anyway? The Lotus chassis was designed to accept various Ford components, sometimes considerably modified, and almost any engine.

The frames were bought by enthusiasts, who acquired the necessary bits and pieces where they could to build up their own cars. Most of them gained competition successes and Colin Chapman assembled one himself with the ubiquitous, side-valve 1172 cc Ford engine. It covered itself with glory, and at a Crystal Palace meeting the reporter for *Motor* described it as 'preposterously fast'.

The Lotus Seven, introduced in 1957, was a logical successor to the Mark 6. The most noticeable changes were the full-width screen above a flat-topped scuttle (the Mark 6 had a raised instrument surround in front of the driver), wishbone front suspension in place of the former divided swing-axles, and a lower and wider radiator grille in a reshaped cowl.

It is here that the author must himself make a brief appearance in the story. After that Crystal Palace meeting in September 1953, I went to Hornsey and borrowed the Mark 6 for the first-ever Lotus road test, which appeared in *Autosport*. The engine was linered down so that it could compete in either the 1100 cc class or in the popular 1172 Formula events, and with twin SU carburettors it probably developed 40 bhp. That doesn't sound much, until you realise that the complete car only weighed $8\frac{1}{2}$ cwt.

With its close-ratio three-speed gearbox it achieved 88 mph in top, 75 mph in second and 40 mph in first. Bottom gear was too high for wheelspin starts, but my acceleration figures were 0–50

mph in 9s, 0–60 mph in 12s, and 0–70 mph in 16s. On a circuit like the Palace, the Lotus could out-corner and out-brake much faster cars, proving that Colin's theories on roadholding and suspension were eminently sound.

The Mark 6 is of the greatest importance because it was the first road-going Lotus that was constructed in any quantity, and the 'productionized' version, the Seven, is still sold by Caterham Car Sales and Coachworks Ltd. as the Super Seven. It can therefore be regarded as the true ancestor of the cars covered by this book. If you drove a Mark 6 you had to dress accordingly, and to enter the car was an acrobatic feat, but the Lotus chassis frame cost £110 and, even if you bought brand new parts (which

10

nobody did), the complete car, with lamps, hood and screen, only set you back £425.

At that time, the Government tried to put a stop to home-built cars and very nearly succeeded in imposing full purchase tax upon them. I formed a committee with Colin Chapman and other interested parties, and we fought tooth-and-nail to prevent this. Luckily, an MP made an incredibly silly speech which played right into our hands. I wrote a blistering reply in *Autosport*, which was read out in the House by another MP — it's all in Hansard. As a result we won the day, and many happy enthusiasts rushed off to Hornsey for their multi-tubular chassis — over 100 as a matter of fact. Lotus have gone far beyond the kit-car stage now, but the tax would have been a crippling blow in those early days.

However, the regulations imposed by the Customs and Excise authority were arduous enough, and as they were to affect Lotus cars right up to the end of the Elan era, perhaps I should summarize the main points, shorn of all their official verbiage. First of all, the generally used expression, 'kit-car', was misleading, though convenient and therefore in common parlance.

In fact, not only was purchase tax chargeable on a complete motor vehicle, but also on a complete kit of parts from which the motor vehicle could be built. Also, the Customs and Excise had the power to decide whether or not a partial kit was what they

There was precious little in common in the appearance of the two Lotus production cars of the late-Fifties. The Elite was arguably the most handsome GT car that had ever been made, while the Seven's uncompromising angularity was an echo from the distant past. The high cost of manufacture of the Elite, however, was to give it only a limited life.

The construction of a body/chassis monocoque out of glass-fibre-reinforced mouldings, with a minimum of help from bonded-in metal components, was ingenious, but unfortunately it was not a technique financially suited to high-volume production. Here are some mouldings in the jig shop of Bristol Aircraft Ltd., who were responsible for many of the Elite monocoques.

called 'substantially a complete kit'. Even a rolling chassis with wheels attached was subject to tax, though it could only be pushed by hand.

Normally, anybody building a motor vehicle was required to register his premises and business activity with the Customs and Excise, when he became subject to all the red tape and bull afflicting car factories. He could avoid registering as a manufacturer, as a concession from the Customs and Excise, only if all the component parts of the car had not been purchased from the same source, and that he received no professional assistance (even an instruction leaflet was taboo!). Above all, the car could not be 'assembled on premises and/or by the use of equipment actually used in the motor trade, *i.e.* retail garage premises and hoists etc'.

So, if you got into difficulties during the assembly and pushed the car round to the local garage for any little job to be done you would automatically become liable for full purchase tax. You would be careful to pump up the tyres by hand, instead of making use of the free air installation, of course!

It was up to the builder of the car to satisfy the local Customs Officer as to the sources where he had obtained the component parts, the premises and equipment used, that he had done the job himself (and any friends who gave him a hand might be quizzed), and that he had not built it 'in the course of trade or by way of business'.

Although the amount of money that was involved was comparatively small, the Customs and Excise thought it worthwhile to employ snoopers, who would stop at nothing to trip up an amateur constructor on some triviality. Perhaps I could tell stories about furtive goings-on in darkened garages, while little men with notebooks listened outside. Perhaps I could, but I won't. The law is an ass, as everybody knows, but asses have long ears, and I do not propose to say anything that might drop somebody in it, even though it all happened a long time ago.

The remarkable thing is that Lotus were able to work out an effective system whereby the parts could be supplied without breaking the law or involving the amateur builder in vexatious litigation. When it came to interpreting the regulations, Colin Chapman had a far keener brain than the little men at the Customs and Excise. As for them, let us hope that their innumerable cups of tea will rot their socks.

It's time to return to the Lotus story, however. After the Mark 6 came the Lotus streamliners, but although I road-tested two Mark 8s, with MG and Coventry Climax engines, and some of their successors, I would scarcely call them sports cars for everyday use. Their body panels were too vulnerable and they were really intended as competition machines.

Incidentally, after Mark 10 it became the practice to describe the cars by a plain number, as 'Lotus Eleven'. The Seven and Super Seven followed this practice because, although they were updated and greatly improved versions of the Mark 6, they did not appear until after the Eleven in 1957. While the Seven was still intended for amateur assembly, such makeshift features as the split Ford front axle had gone, the Formula 2 wishbone suspension being used, and Colin Chapman's designs were becoming altogether more mature.

The car that really put Louts on the map, and also nearly bankrupted the young firm, was the original Elite. The object was to produce the ultimate in GT cars, but whereas the Elite proved to be enormously successful in racing, it never attained a great reputation as a road-going car. The public were unsure of the name, Lotus, associating it with extremely fast sports-racing and racing cars. That could in time have been overcome if the Elite had proved to be a sturdy and reliable workhorse, but this it never was.

What the Elite did was to demonstrate that Lotus had made a giant's stride forward, and its appearance at the 1957 Motor Show at Earls Court did more for the prestige of the firm than all the racing successes put together. Here was an ultra-modern GT car, beautiful and infinitely desirable, and if it had been assembled in a tremendous hurry, minus a few essential organs that didn't show from the outside, nobody would have guessed it.

The previous Lotus models had appeared to the public to be impractical, road-going specials, which were enormous fun to drive at weekends, provided that you didn't mind a few spots of oil on your trousers and mud on your right elbow. The Elite, on the other hand, looked like an ideal businessman's express, which would not seem out of place in the Director's car park.

Let us briefly recall the design of the Elite. It had a glass-fibre body shell, which was not unusual among cars in limited production. What was entirely new was the use of the body as a chassis, bearing all the stresses and loads that would normally be taken by a separate frame. The structure was thickened, or reinforced with steel, at the mounting points for the suspension assemblies, but this was a true glass-fibre monocoque, cleverly reinforced by a series of built-in boxes.

The car was powered by an overhead-camshaft Coventry Climax engine of 1216 cc, in effect an enlarged FWA 1100 cc unit. This size was chosen to suit the 1300 cc Grand Touring class in races, and although it was small it coped easily with the incredibly light weight of 11 cwt, which was the reward for using such unconventional methods of construction. The BMC gearbox and the hypoid final drive were at least proprietary components with plenty of development behind them.

The suspension came straight from the Formula 2 single-seater and there were disc brakes all round, which was still more akin to racing practice than to normal production in those days.

The Elite was a graceful car from any angle, in this instance the smooth line of the waist being emphasized by a darker colouring for the upper section of the body. The neatly laid-out instrument panel can be seen clearly through the rear screen.

Centre-locking wire wheels contributed to the appearance and to brake cooling. Truly, this seemed to be the car for which everybody had been waiting, with such performance, roadholding and looks as had never been available before. It was a far cry from DIY specials, and if many Elites were, in fact, assembled by their owners to avoid purchase tax, this was mentioned in hushed tones.

Though the real production Elite did not appear until the Motor Show of 1958, a few pre-production cars were raced during that season. Of these, Ian Walker's machine was incredibly successful, winning its class everywhere it went.

Unfortunately, the Elite was too nearly a racing car and as a road car it proved far too noisy and unrefined. Colin Chapman had become a brilliant designer, perhaps *the* most brilliant designer, of competition cars, but he knew little of the hard facts of costing for a production run, nor had he any experience of quality control.

That some of the road-going Elites ran into Problems, with a capital P, would be an understatement, but the biggest headache was that the car proved too expensive to build. Lotus moved to a new and larger factory at Cheshunt in June 1959, where they were to remain for seven years. There, the quality problems of road-going Elites were sorted out, but the car was still too close to racing to be a real production job.

Everybody at Lotus, and Colin Chapman in particular, now realised that the series-production of GT cars was a vastly different exercise from the hand-building of racing cars. Though the Elite was greatly improved, it was being subsidised by the racing side of the business. It transpired afterwards that the Elite had lost the firm something like £100 per car, but the money was far from wasted.

The experience gained from the adventure all went into a new road-going Lotus. It was as simple to produce as its predecessor had been difficult and it had the comfort and refinement which the Elite had lacked. To many of us it was the ultimate small sports car, with a charm which nothing before or since has ever quite equalled. It was announced at the Earls Court Motor Show of 1962, the new Lotus Elan.

CHAPTER 2

The Twin-Cam engine

First take a Ford 1500

Colin Chapman has never really regarded himself as an engine man, which is probably one of the reasons why all the early Lotus cars had proprietary power units. After the Austin Seven, there were the immortal side-valve 1172 cc Ford and the later 105E, the pushrod MG XPAG and the good but expensive Coventry Climax with a single overhead camshaft, among others.

Nevertheless, when ideas for the future Elan were forming in Colin's fertile brain, a suitable engine at a reasonable price just did not exist. If he wanted a twin-cam unit that was light, powerful and refined he would have to produce it himself. He realised that the bottom end of a short-stroke Ford engine would have ample reserves of strength, but what about the all-important cylinder-head?

It is at this point that Harry Mundy enters the story. Harry was a very experienced designer, who had worked on the BRM, designed Coventry Climax engines, and was later to be deeply involved in the production of the 12-cylinder Jaguar, but at that particular period he was the Technical Editor of *Autocar*. It so happened that he had been sharpening his pencil on a new twin-cam design for the Facellia sports car, but Facel Vega were already getting short of money and the project fell through. Thus, he had already done a lot of preliminary work that enabled him to design a twin-cam cylinder-head in double-quick time. Incidentally, there was also to be a Mundy-designed Formula 1 Facel, which was stillborn.

In broad terms, the original light-alloy Mundy head was arranged for bolting down on to the bottom half of a 1500 cc

Ford engine. In front, a single roller chain drove the twin overhead camshafts and also embraced the sprocket of the existing side camshaft, of which the cams rotated idly with no tappets to operate. This extra camshaft was far from redundant, however, for its skew gears were required to drive the distributor and the oil pump, while the cam for the fuel pump was still operational. A jockey sprocket was pressed against the upward run of the chain, with an external adjustment to set the tension.

The preliminary testing was carried out on a stretched 109E block, nominally of 1340 cc, but then the much stronger, five-bearing 116E Cortina engine became available, for which the head was redesigned. In any case, it had proved insufficiently rigid, and distortion of the face had sometimes allowed the gasket to blow. External webs were therefore cast across the central depression between the camshaft housings and within the water jackets to relieve the stresses of the combustion chambers. These worked rather like the stays around the firebox in a locomotive boiler and they converted an excessively flexible head into one that was more rigid than the standard cast-iron job. The housing for the camshaft chain had also to be extended to match the taller block.

Although Lotus had recently moved from Tottenham Lane, Hornsey, to Delamere Road, Cheshunt, they still lacked the machine-shop capacity to undertake the manufacture of the new engine themselves. Luckily, Colin Chapman was familiar with the firm of J. A. Prestwich, situated close to his former premises, which made the famous JAP engines. They installed the necessary machinery for producing the light-alloy heads, also assembling and bench-testing the engines.

Later, JAP were taken over by Villiers and all the machine tools were transferred to Wolverhampton. Unfortunately, there were the usual industrial problems of that area and production failed to keep pace with demand. So, when Lotus moved again to Hethel, they acquired the complete outfit of jigs and tools from Villiers and set up a machine shop for the twin-cam engine. Let us shed a tear for the JAP factory at Tottenham, from which so many splendid engines had emerged during well over half a century; it descended to the manufacture of pencils, but that is getting ahead of the story.

The original Lotus 1500 cc twin-cam engine, after much bench-testing and many road miles under the bonnets of some most unlikely-looking cars, went into production at Tottenham in the summer of 1962. It was therefore ready for the introduction of the Elan at the Motor Show in October. About 22 Elans were delivered with this engine and then, for some obscure reason, the international class was increased to 1600 cc for competition purposes.

It was therefore decided to enlarge the cylinder bore, the resulting dimensions being 82.55 × 72.75 mm (1558 cc). The blocks were still the basic 1500 cc five-bearing components, but selected by Fords as having enough 'meat' for over-boring. There is, of course, some permitted variation in the best foundry work, especially in cast-iron, and so an occasional lucky one came through that was judged safe for boring out to almost the full 1600 cc. These carried a special identification mark and were reserved for racing. The first 22 Elans are all believed to have been converted to the larger capacity, but having driven both types I did not notice any appreciable difference.

There were two different types of cylinder-head castings, both of which had similar combustion chambers and exhaust ports. One had four separate inlet ports, for use with two Weber or Dellorto twin-choke carburettors, but the other had siamesed inlets and was intended for use with two Zenith-Stromberg constant-vacuum instruments. The latter head was produced for countries, such as the USA, which demanded low exhaust emissions, but it was also sold for a period in the UK.

For the USA, an elaborate arrangement was developed in which a device known as a 'throttle body' was sandwiched between the carburettors and the ports, containing an extra throttle for each carburettor, and two pipes passed right over the engine to take the mixture to and from a hot spot on the exhaust manifold. When the Zenith-Stromberg carburettors were supplied for use in Britain, the throttle body and the cross-over pipes were omitted.

Both types of cylinder-head were available with alternative compression ratios of 9.5:1 (standard) or 10.3:1 (Sprint), and they were stamped S or H respectively for identification. The gasket face of the head was machined with a carbide-tipped multi-bladed milling cutter and for the higher compression ratio, 40 thou more metal was removed; the combustion chambers were also fully machined. For normal, road-going Elans a copper-asbestos gasket was employed.

The valves were at an angle of 27° to the vertical and operated in replaceable cast-iron guides and seats. The double valve springs were secured by Ford collets and split cotters. Bucket-type tappets enveloped the valve springs and the clearances were adjusted by changing the shims. At first, the tappets ran directly in the aluminium, but it was found that dirt tended to be held by the soft metal and act as an abrasive against the tappets. A small redesign was therefore carried out. Cast-iron sleeves were inserted in the head (from engine No. LP 1576), which was heated to 150°C (302°F). After insertion, the sleeves were fine-bored in position by a machine with four boring heads.

The valve guides were pressed into position and located by circlips, with the head at 100°/150°C (212°/303°F), after which they were reamed. The valve seats were frozen in dry ice at −80°C (−112°F) and inserted with a special tool, with the head at a temperature not exceeding 200°C (392°F), after which the seatings were re-cut. It will be understood that in the case of a new engine, all these operations could be performed at a single heating.

The camshafts each ran in five steel-backed white-metal bearings and end location was by a shoulder in front, against the head. The jackshaft (ex-camshaft) was in three similar bearings and was located by a thrust plate bolted to the front face of the cylinder-block. The jockey sprocket for the single-row roller

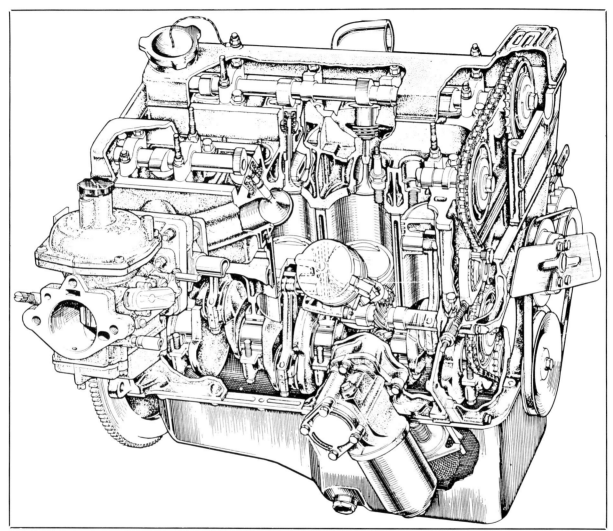

This cutaway drawing of the Lotus twin-cam engine shows the long roller chain that drives the camshafts. It also embraces the sprocket of the jackshaft, which drives the distributor, oil pump and petrol pump, the ex-Ford cams being redundant. The adjustment for the spring-loaded jockey sprocket can also be seen. This particular engine has the two-port head for Stromberg carburettors.

timing chain was on a spring-loaded rocker, with a screw adjustment outside the aluminium case.

The cast-iron, dynamically balanced crankshaft ran in five steel-backed lead-bronze bearings in aluminium caps, with two bolts and ring dowels. It was located by split thrust washers on either side of the centre main bearing, which was notched for extra oil supply to the more heavily loaded rear washer that resisted the end-thrust from the clutch. There were two types of crankshaft with different flanges, the early ones having the flywheel attached by four bolts and the later ones by six. Note that a different type of oil seal must be used with the latter shaft. The flywheel was of cast-iron with a shrunk-on steel starter ring.

At first, the steel H-section connecting-rods were Lotus products, but Ford later introduced rods that were considered equally good. They had steel-backed bronze little-end bushes and copper-lead big-end bearings in steel shells, each cap being located by a pair of dowels and secured by two bolts. The solid-skirt pistons had their gudgeon pins retained by circlips and carried two compression and one oil-control ring, all above the gudgeon. Note that the later type of oil-control ring, with an expander ring and two rails, cannot be fitted with a ring-compressing tool.

The oil pump, of the eccentric bi-rotor type, was bolted to the right side of the block and driven by the skew gear on the jackshaft, as previously described. Its housing contained a non-adjustable relief valve, set for 40/45 lb pressure, and with new bearings the gauge would show 35 lb at 2,000 rpm. The pump drew oil from the sump and passed it through a full-flow filter to a short oil gallery on the right side of the engine, with a transmitter for the oil-pressure gauge at its forward end. At the rear end, a cross-drilling took the oil to the main gallery at the other side of the engine, from which all the main crankshaft bearings were fed. The big-ends received their oil from drillings in the front, centre and rear main journals; the pistons and gudgeon pins were lubricated both by oil mist and from small jets in the connecting-rod webs.

The three jackshaft bearings were connected to the front, centre and rear mains by cross-drillings through the block, while a metered jet looked after the chain and sprockets. From the front jackshaft bearing, oil was fed upwards through the gasket to the front right-hand camshaft bearing, and through a cross-drilling in the head to the left-hand one. Its flow was controlled by flats machined on the jackshaft front journal. It passed through the hollow shafts to the other bearings and cams, the rear-ends of the shafts being sealed with tapered Allen screws. Having done its work upstairs, the lubricant was led back to the sump by a collecting box and a rubber tube. Vintage purists might deplore the pressed-steel sump, but even Rolls-Royce are using them now, for ease of repair in distant places.

The water-pump housing was integral with the timing cover, the lower hose from the right-hand side of the radiator being connected to a pipe which was part of the aluminium casting. The chain was situated between the timing cover and a back-plate, which was sandwiched between the cover and the cylinder-block. The water pump located in the backplate and its impellor operated in a depression machined in the front of the block, from which the water was directed upwards through the gasket to cool the head. There was a projection on the left side of the head which contained the thermostat and the sensor for the temperature gauge. This projection was formed into the water outlet, to which the hose from the top of the radiator was attached.

The shaft, on which the impellor was mounted, carried a slinger and passed through a seal, with a pulley on its forward end for a vee-belt drive from the crankshaft pulley. Elans generally had a small, two-bladed metal fan mounted on the water-pump pulley, though a multi-bladed plastic fan was also available. The +2 and Europa had electric fans, as did the last Elans. The Elan always had a dynamo (DC generator) driven by the fan belt, and it is worth noting that early cars had a positive earth connection, the change to negative occurring after chassis No 7894. The +2 and Europa were fitted with alternators. The Elan Series 1 and S2 had a relatively narrow radiator with a very thick matrix, with blanking plates on either side to direct the air through it, but S3 and S4 had a wider (Triumph Spitfire) radiator, of which there were two types.

There were three types of camshaft, apart from the fancy ones from engine tuners. The B shaft had a plain boss for the sprocket, the C shaft had a groove machined in the boss, and the D shaft had two grooves for identification purposes. The S1, 2 and 3 Elans were normally fitted with a B camshaft and two twin-choke Weber carburettors, with a claimed power output of 105 bhp.

In January 1966, the Special Equipment version of the Elan became available, which had the C camshaft and developed 115 bhp with the Webers. The D camshaft was first used with two Zenith-Stromberg carburettors, and all the emission equipment previously described, for the USA market. It was then found that the Strombergs gave results comparable with the Webers, with the throttle bodies and crossover pipes to the hot-spot removed, using adaptor blocks and a balance pipe, the head being of the type with siamesed inlet ports.

This arrangement was adopted for all Elans except the +2S in November 1968, but it was found desirable to let a little warm air into the flexible trunking as the Strombergs were prone to icing. To improve idling, the balance-pipe was mounted higher up in the adaptor blocks, but although the Strombergs were alleged to give as much power as the Webers, the engines fitted with them did not seem to rev so readily, and they were not popular. After less than a year, the factory reverted to four carburettor chokes, a modification which some owners had already carried out.

When Tony Rudd introduced his Big Valve engine, which developed 126 bhp, he used the eight-port head. At first the Weber carburettors did not work well with the D camshaft, and Tony fitted two Dellorto twin-choke instruments, but later some new settings were found for the Webers and the old favourites were reinstated. The Federal (USA) engines had a distributor capsule giving 5° retard for idling, which was also found on the Big Valve engines, but some owners preferred to disconnect it. An AC fuel pump, driven by a cam on the jack-shaft, was used on all engines.

Half-a-dozen different types of exhaust manifolds were used during the life of the Twin-Cam engine. Originally, a cast-iron manifold which mated with a single downpipe was employed, but Special Equipment cars had a divided manifold, also cast, which was attached to a double downpipe by flanges and three bolts. This was prone to blown exhaust joints and it was replaced by a later version, which was not much better.

Cast-iron manifolds were standard on S1, 2 and 3 Elans, but the divided manifold was gradually dropped for Special Equipment cars in favour of two fabricated tubular manifolds, one serving cylinders 1 and 4, the other 2 and 3. These were integral with their downpipes, which remained separate until they swept into a horizontal position, where they were united by a Y box. These tubular manifolds were standard on the Elan Sprint and the +2 and were often fitted to earlier cars. The other two manifolds were cast-iron and provided a hot spot to which the flanges of the crossover pipes of Federal engines were bolted; they differed in details only.

The single downpipe carried a small expansion chamber below the manifold and the main silencer was mounted cross-wise at the rear of the car. There were two types, which differed principally in their piping arrangements, and then a pair of cylindrical silencers were mounted fore and aft, side by side. Finally, a single oval silencer, also fore and aft, was used; the small expansion chamber was not found on twin downpipes. The +2 had an oval silencer, at first crosswise and later in the conventional position, with a heat shield above it in both cases.

Many Elans were raced with the standard cast-iron crank-shaft, but the engines prepared by the tuning specialists had steel cranks with nitralloy-hardened journals. Oil coolers were not considered necessary for road work, but they were always used for racing. Some of the works cars had a Cosworth bottom-end and a cylinder-head that had received the treatment from BRM.

It might be said that the Twin-Cam engine had humble beginnings and was of the greatest simplicity. Nevertheless, it was generally extremely reliable and had a very long life, while it could be reconditioned by a mechanically-minded owner without a lot of special tools. Both on the road and on the circuits it earned a splendid reputation.

CHAPTER 3

The Elan

Backbone to success

The racing car of today is the touring car of tomorrow. That ancient *cliché*, probably of Edwardian origin, is still trotted out by tired journalists who are trying to fill their allotted space. It's true, up to a point, for the superior handling and roadholding of the Lotus single-seaters must rub off on to the production cars built in the same factory. Nevertheless, there are many characteristics of the competition car which are totally irrelevant to road-going models, and great *marques* have perished in the past because that distinction was not observed.

It could have happened to the young Lotus Company in the case of the Elite. The original intention was that this should be *the* sophisticated GT coupé, for which there was considerable demand. In fact, it turned out to be a detuned racer, which paid scant regard to the silence and refinement that even sport cars were beginning to offer. In a few words, it was too expensive to make and its many racing triumphs did not compensate those owners who found that they had acquired a noisy and temperamental car.

On the other hand, the Mark 6 was a complete success, because it was the ultimate fun car, but although almost every motoring enthusiast thinks that he wants a doorless open two-seater, when it comes to signing the cheque he usually chooses something more luxurious. The Elan had therefore to be a genuine sports car that was a practical production job, with the ride and refinement of any good saloon. A certain percentage of the cars would have folding hoods instead of hardtops, but complete weather protection was required in either case.

The use of a glass-fibre body shell as a monocoque had not been trouble-free, and although the more serious problems had been overcome, there was some prejudice against the principle. In any case, a monocoque, whether plastic or pressed steel, relies on its roof for much of its rigidity and it becomes far too heavy if it has to be reinforced to allow the top to be opened. The apertures for the doors weaken the structure still further and we are all too familiar with open cars that are martyrs to scuttle shake.

Fundamentally, therefore, the glass-fibre body had to be independent of the main stress-bearing chassis, as extreme rigidity is essential for suspension and roadholding of the Lotus calibre. A multi-tubular spaceframe could not be used as it would obstruct the doors, but a 'ladder' frame, box-section or consisting of two jolly great tubes, would have been hopelessly heavy and old-fashioned. An American designer once claimed that he would 'simplicate and add lightness', and that is what Colin Chapman did.

In car design, it's as likely as not that the newest idea was originally used, and then forgotten, many years ago. You have only to look at the veterans on the Brighton Run to realise the truth of that assertion. So, when Colin Chapman built his first experimental backbone chassis for the Elan he was breaking no new ground. However, his backbone was not the circular tube of the 1905 Rover, the Austro-Daimler, the Alpine and countless others, but pressed-steel sheet of 16 and 18 Gauge, welded into a rectangular girder 11 inches deep.

It is said that he was so impressed with the lightness and rigidity of the Elan that he at once started to translate the idea

The first Lotus Elans had convertible bodywork and were powered by a 1498 cc version of the twin-cam engine, hence the 'Elan 1500' badge above the leading edge of the doors. This particular car, photographed during a brief road test at Zandvoort, was used for a time by Jim Clark.

into Formula 1 terms. Whereas the Elan had a separate body, which sat on the backbone like a saddle with the occupants either side, the single-seater version had an enlarged backbone, with a hole through which the driver could climb.

So, the steel backbone of the Elan became the light-alloy monocoque of the Lotus 25, which was eventually copied by every Formula 1 constructor, and while you and I knew that Gabriel Voisin had built light-alloy monocoques for the 1923 French Grand Prix, Colin Chapman didn't! In any case, whether or not you accept the similarity of the Formula 1 Lotus 25 and the road-going Lotus 26 Elan, they both burst upon an astonished world in 1962.

Like all the best engineering, the chassis of the Elan was extraordinarily simple. Fabricated by CO_2 welding from mild-steel pressings, the rectangular central section was relatively narrow and acted as the propeller-shaft tunnel. Pierced for lightness, it separated in front into a two-pronged fork which embraced the engine and gearbox, the two forward ends being welded to a box-section cross-member terminating in integral uprights. These accommodated the upper ends of the coil springs and dampers, also the pivots for the top wishbones of the front suspension. The lower pivot points were on the cross-member itself, which also carried the rack-and-pinion steering.

At the rear, the central section split into a much shorter fork, again united by a cross-member and a pair of uprights, taller in this case. These received the upper ends of the suspension struts, on Lotocone mountings, and the final-drive casing was suspended beneath the cross-member, on rubber mountings, with two torque rods underneath running forward to the chassis. In addition to the fork, the bottom panel of the central

This was Jim Clark's second Elan, which, like its predecessor, passed into the hands of his great friend Ian Scott Watson, seen here shortly after taking delivery. It is a Series 1 convertible with the optional hardtop, the only way you could order a closed Elan before the advent of the coupe in 1965.

Rear view of the ex-Clark Elan 1600 hardtop. The separate stop lights and traffic indicators identify this as one of the earlier Elans.

different points. For the Elan, the thickness only depended on the necessary reserve of strength to resist the use and misuse to which the body of any sports car may be subjected by its occupants; racing shells could consequently be of far lighter construction, with fewer laminations.

The chassis arrived in red oxide paint and then received a bitumastic covering, the large lightening holes making it easy to paint the interior of the closed central section. In any case, corrosion of such a sturdy structure was far less likely than of a typical pressed-steel body, with thin panels concealing many inaccessible spots. The glass-fibre shell fitted over the backbone like a saddle, to which it was secured by some 16 bolts, and it could easily be removed for any necessary repairs — a useful provision for some of the hairier sports car drivers! Sound deadening material was sandwiched between the chassis and the body.

The body shell was in one piece, but it started off as separate upper and lower sections in the early stages of construction. The main shape was built up in one mould, while the floor pan and wheel-arches were formed in the other. During construction, the two moulds were brought together and the body was formed into a one-piece moulding by lamination at the seams. To those unfamiliar with these methods, it should perhaps be explained that such a joint can be as strong as any other part of the moulding, so this really was a one-piece body, quickly detach-able from the main chassis.

Once again, we come up against those tricky door apertures, always a problem in any sort of body. In the case of the Elan, steel frames were welded up and incorporated in the mouldings, which also provided extra stiffening for the outer seat mountings, pedal supports and safety-belt anchorages.

In general, the body was constructed of 2.4 oz chopped strand mat, using a high-quality Polyester for the layup, giving a panel thickness for a standard road-going car of $\frac{1}{8}$ in (3.17 mm), increasing to $\frac{1}{4}$ in (6.35 mm) at major structural attachment points. The bolts for securing the shell to the chassis were received in bobbins, usually threaded internally and of four different sizes, according to their duties. Where the bobbins were inserted in the moulding, it was built up by extra lamina-

section was also extended to the rear, with light tubular bracing upwards to the cross-member. This was to carry the lugs for the pivot points of the wishbones, which had to be placed as low as possible in conjunction with the high-mounted Chapman struts.

The steel backbone chassis of the Elan was at first a product of John Thompson's Motor Pressings, but subsequently Lotus took over its manufacture themselves; they still retain all the jigs for ensuring the correct alignments, and small batches of frames are made from time to time for replacement purposes! The glass-fibre body shell was far easier to manufacture than that of the Elite because it was virtually an unstressed member, though contributing incidentally to the torsional stiffness when bolted down. In the case of the Elite, the exact thickness of the glass-fibre was crucial to the rigidity of the structure and varied at

The backbone chassis, a design concept which was not only the basis of the Elan, and subsequently of the Europa and Plus 2, but which also inspired Colin Chapman to create his Lotus 25 monocoque Grand Prix car in 1962, even before the Elan had been unveiled to the public; it was a question of spacing the side members far enough apart to leave room for a driver between them.

24

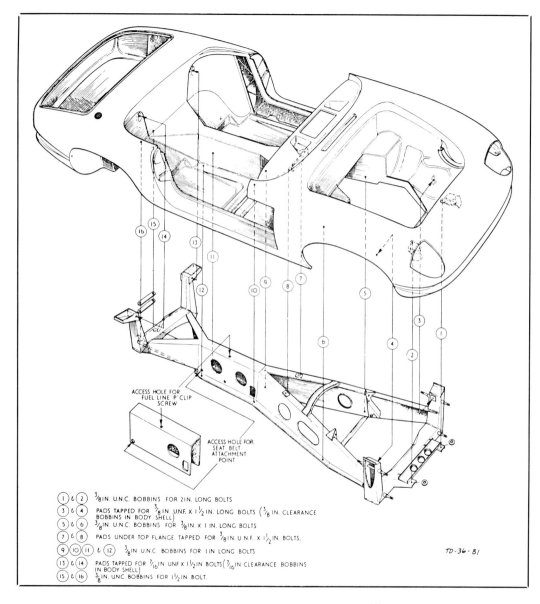

This drawing shows how the one-piece glass-fibre body of the Elan forms a saddle to fit over the steel backbone chassis, to which it is bolted at 16 points. Sound-deadening material is placed between the two units and the mounting bolts fit into bobbins which are situated in strengthened sections of the body. The body shell is not a stressed member, though it does confer some extra stiffening of the structure.

ACCESS HOLE FOR
FUEL LINE P'CLIP
SCREW

ACCESS HOLE FOR
SEAT BELT
ATTACHMENT
POINT

① & ② ³/₈IN. U.N.C. BOBBINS FOR 2IN. LONG BOLTS

③ & ④ PADS TAPPED FOR ³/₈ IN. UNF. X 1½ IN. LONG BOLTS (³/₈ IN. CLEARANCE BOBBINS IN BODY SHELL)

⑤ & ⑥ ³/₈IN. U.N.C. BOBBINS FOR ³/₈ IN. X 1 IN. LONG BOLTS

⑦ & ⑧ PADS UNDER TOP FLANGE TAPPED FOR ³/₈IN. U.N.F. X 1½ IN. BOLTS.

⑨ ⑩ ⑪ & ⑫ ³/₈IN U.N.C BOBBINS FOR 1IN LONG BOLTS

⑬ & ⑭ PADS TAPPED FOR ⁷/₁₆IN UNF X 1½ IN BOLTS (⁷/₁₆IN CLEARANCE BOBBINS IN BODY SHELL)

⑮ & ⑯ ³/₈IN. UNC BOBBINS FOR 1½ IN BOLT.

TD-36-81

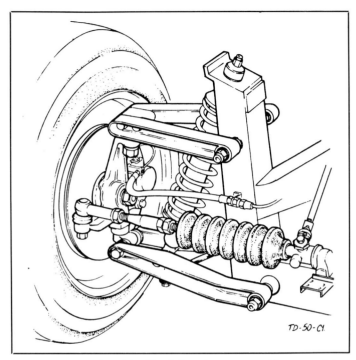

The front suspension of the Elan is largely constructed from proprietary parts. The unequal-length wishbones can be seen, with spring/damper unit and rack-and-pinion steering, but the anti-roll bar is not clearly visible in this case.

tions, arranged to give continuity of flow. Where necessary, panel stiffening was achieved with double-skinned areas or box sections.

The glass-fibre bodies of Elans were not self-coloured but painted externally. The process presented a few problems initially, but after Polyurethane primer-surfacer was adopted the results were most satisfactory. The paint procedure was quite lengthy, with many intermediate cleaning and drying processes, but perhaps it can be summarized by saying that there were two applications of primer, rubbed down with wet 320 or 360 grade paper, followed by the first colour coat, flatted with wet 400

paper and then thoroughly washed. The final colour coat, after force drying for 50 minutes, was rectified with 600 paper, polished with coarse then fine compound, and finished with Pinchin and Johnson liquid wax polish.

Wherever possible, proprietary parts that were already in production were adopted, to reduce the cost; the lessons of the Elite had been well and truly learned. The front suspension uprights, with ball-joints at the top and trunnions below, were by Alford and Alder, as were the stub axles, steering arms and rack-and-pinion assembly, but the pressed-steel wishbones were special Lotus components. The rack had rubber mountings and the suspension bushes were also rubber, for this was to be a refined road car and such crudities as bump thump and road noise must not be transmitted into the interior. Naturally, these rubbers were deleted from cars intended for racing. The front telescopic dampers and springs were Armstrong products, but the anti-roll bar was specially made.

At the rear, MacPherson struts, also of Armstrong manufacture, were shrunk into special aluminium housings, each containing two ball-races and the live stub-axles carrying the hubs. Later Elans had the larger inner races that were also found on the +2. As previously mentioned, the struts were seated in Lotocone rubber bushes, held by the vertical extensions at the ends of the rear cross-member. The bottom wishbones were wide-based, welded up from steel tubes and triangulated. They had bonded-rubber bushes at each end, the inboard ones being held in lugs welded to the lower chassis extension (again, no rubber for racing).

The drive-shafts carried Rotoflex rubber doughnut-type universal joints, both the differential shafts and live stub-axles having integral three-legged spiders, similar to those on the tubular fixed-length drive-shafts. The first Elan prototype had inboard rear brakes, but these had to be abandoned because of the well-known propensity of the doughnuts for winding up and unwinding. This allowed the car to roll for appreciable distances in both directions with the handbrake firmly applied, which could be awkward when parking, especially on a gradient.

The original doughnuts, though stiffer than those used by Triumph, still allowed a disagreeable surging to take place at

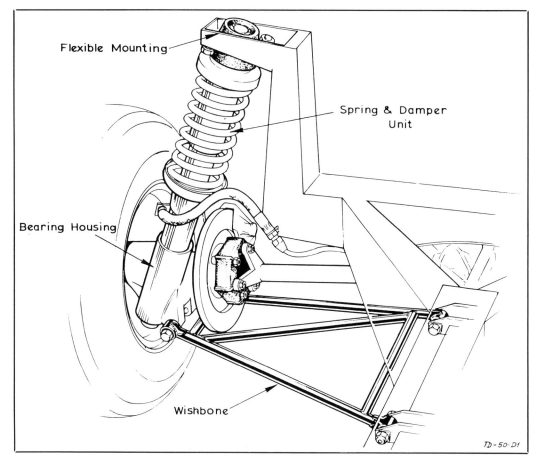

The Elan has strut-type independent rear suspension, with wide-based lower wishbone of triangulated tubular construction. The brake discs are mounted remotely from the wheels, on the inner ends of the live stub-axles, and one of the rubber doughnut universal joints is visible in this drawing.

Flexible Mounting

Spring & Damper Unit

Bearing Housing

Wishbone

TD-50-D1

low speeds if care was not exercised in throttle control. A later version, with metallic reinforcement, was far better in this respect.

There was some prejudice against the Rotoflex couplings, caused by the surging that was experienced with the earlier type, but they had very real advantages and perhaps it would be permissible to interject a few words on their behalf. The orthodox drive-shaft of commerce, with two Hooke's universal-joints and a splined slip-joint, was the unsuspected cause of poor roadholding in many cars with independent or De Dion rear suspension systems. The splined slip-joint could offer unwanted friction to the action of the suspension, or even jam under load; this could cause vicious rear-end breakaway when cornering and actual seizure was not unknown.

The doughnut joint had a period of popularity in racing, even in Formula 1, and it acted incidentally as a very efficient trans-

So as to avoid the burden of Purchase Tax, potential Elan owners could opt to buy their car in component form, although as part of the arrangement they were not allowed to enlist any professional help in assembly. Britain at that time seemed to be particularly well endowed with enthusiastic and talented amateurs!

mission shock-absorber, allowing transmissions to be used in some cases which proved insufficiently strong when orthodox drive-shafts were employed. More sophisticated drive-shafts, with roller-bearing slip-joints, subsequently ousted the cheap, light and simple Rotoflex joints for racing cars. Incidentally, some racing Elans had orthodox drive-shafts.

Once again, standard production parts were employed as far as possible in the final-drive assembly. The nosepiece came from a Ford rear axle, but instead of bolting up to a pressed-steel live-axle banjo, it was fitted to a special light-alloy housing. This had two arms, upon which it was suspended on rubber mountings from the rear chassis cross-member, which took the weight and absorbed the torque reaction from the pinion. The major reaction from the crownwheel was fed into the central backbone by two torque rods, rubber insulated of course, from lugs cast on either side beneath the housing.

The hypoid crownwheel and pinion were available in 3.9, 3.77 and 3.55:1 ratios and a two-star bevel-gear differential was considered adequate to handle the torque of the twin-cam engine. An oil-level plug was situated in the rear of the light-alloy housing, and a drain plug was a refinement which some Ford axles lacked.

The propeller shaft ran within the steel backbone and had no axle movements to absorb. It was of normal tubular construction, and though endowed with Hooke's joints at both ends it had only to accommodate fractional misalignments. At first glance it would appear that there was no provision for telescopic accommodation, but in fact there was a concealed slip-joint in the housing at the rear of the gearbox, ahead of the front universal joint. This slip-joint was on inverted splines and was lubricated from the gearbox.

The gearbox was also a Ford component, with synchromesh on all four speeds. Two sets of ratios were available, which affected the overall length of the box and hence that of the propeller shaft, which was listed in two lengths. The clutch was a standard Borg and Beck component, with hydraulic operation.

The last five or six Elans produced had the five-speed box of the +2, but this modification was never catalogued, though it was something that the Elan had always needed, particularly for long-distance Continental touring. It must be remembered, however, that the motorway mileage in Great Britain was relatively small when the Elan was designed, and therefore fairly low gearing was acceptable, to the benefit of rapid overtaking.

Fierce acceleration calls for brakes to match and there were outboard discs on all four wheels. Actually, the term 'outboard' might be misconstrued in relation to the rear brakes, for the discs and the two-cylinder Girling calipers were not adjacent to the wheels but were mounted on the inboard side of the bearings, close to the Rotoflex couplings. However, they were, of course, unsprung, and by inboard brakes we usually mean those which are attached to the sprung mass of the car.

The handbrake had a mechanical hook-up of typical Girling type, with rods in tension, operating on the upper pads of the rear discs. The front brakes were conventionally mounted and very similar to those at the rear, though minus the handbrake linkage; larger calipers were used from Series 2 onwards.

A single master-cylinder was normally used, with an integral

It was probably the exceptional roadholding of Lotus cars generally which encouraged one or two Police forces to take a close look at the Elan. This is a Series 2 convertible with a clear message on the nose; a similar sticker, on the boot lid, came into view after you had been overtaken!

Although strictly speaking a two-seater, the Elan caused Lotus to experiment with a child's seat perched on top of the chassis backbone in the hope of giving the car more family appeal; most people elected to wait for the Plus 2.

ible to state which Series did or did not have the servo, and whether or not it was confined to the so-called Special Equipment models. Actually, the servo was first offered in January 1966 as part of the Special Equipment package, but that is an over-simplification.

Although the Elan was catalogued as a complete car, hardly any were sold in that form, and virtually all the purchasers elected to assemble their vehicles at home, thus escaping purchase tax. Though many of them started out with basic kits, they generally decided at some point to add various Special Equipment items as they went along. One could almost say that, in practice, there was no such animal as a bog-standard Elan. It would appear that most of the cars eventually had servos, whether they were built with them or had them added later, though the plain, non-servo brakes were perfectly adequate, and none of the first Elans had them from new. Cars fitted with the servo used harder brake pads, and Lotus supplied the correct type with the servo kit.

The engine-gearbox unit was mounted between the arms of the front chassis fork. Two brackets were formed on the inside of these arms, to carry the rubber insulation blocks which supported the cylinder casting on either side. At the rear, a mounting plate was bolted up to the chassis fork and supported the back of the gearbox, which again rested on a rubber block, the gearbox extension penetrating the tunnel formed by the central backbone.

A fabricated support for the steering rack-and-pinion was welded on the forward face of the main cross-member locating the front suspension. One of the greatest attractions of the Lotus Elan was the very quick steering, with only $2\frac{1}{2}$ turns of the steering wheel from lock to lock. This gave admirable control and exceptionally sensitive appreciation of road-surface conditions, felt by the driver at the rim of the steering wheel.

On the other hand, such high-geared and precise steering could be particularly subject to careless assembly, which would affect the geometry. In particular, the height of the rack was critical, and the apparently simple task of mounting it could only be carried out with the aid of a jig and a suitable selection of shims. Quite a small error could introduce bump-steer effects,

reservoir and a simple hydraulic circuit, which included a pressure-differential warning valve. This was connected to a red light on the instrument panel, which glowed if all was not well, and there was a test switch for verification of the bulb at regular intervals (not fitted to all Elans). For some export markets, dual circuits were already compulsory, and there was an alternative assembly with tandem master-cylinders.

A vacuum-operated servo could be fitted to the braking system, and this was merely connected in series on the pressure side of the master-cylinder. There were two types of servo, the earlier one being piston-operated while the final version contained the diaphragm with which one is now familiar.

Perhaps it would be permissible to interrupt the description again with a small red herring. Theoretically, it would be poss-

Three views of a Special Equipment Series 2 Elan, usually identifiable by its centre-lock wheels (though these were a listed option for the standard model) and by 'Elan S/E' badges about a foot to the rear of the traffic indicator repeater lights. By this time the rear lighting arrangements had been gathered into two clusters.

which were totally absent when the geometry was spot-on.

The radiator was situated above the rack-and-pinion steering gear. At the same time as the Zenith-Stromberg carburettors were introduced, an electric fan was fitted ahead of the matrix, secured by brackets bolted to either side of the radiator, and this was often added by owners to earlier models. It was controlled by a thermal switch, situated either in the header tank or the upper hose connection, for which there was a special adaptor. The Sprint model had a deflector plate beneath the radiator, to collect more air, and this was often fitted to earlier cars, cooling tending to be marginal. Later cars had a recuperator bottle, piped to the neck of the filler cap.

The fuel tank, containing $9\frac{1}{4}$ Imperial gallons, was situated at the rear of the luggage boot. The filler neck was in the right-hand rear body panel and was coupled to the tank by a short flexible hose. For some foreign markets it was necessary to connect a catch-tank to the filler neck and the tank was vented to a canister containing a purifying chemical. The electrical gauge unit was in the rear face of the tank and connected to the gauge on the facia, current being supplied via the ignition switch.

The petrol pipe ran from the bottom of the tank to an AC pump on the right side of the engine, operated by the jackshaft. The petrol filter was attached to the pump and the air filter for the carburettors was ahead of the radiator.

While the front hubs had taper roller bearings, those at the rear had ball races. Steel wheels were standard and there were two types of these, the centre-locking pattern with knock-on hub caps, which was an option from Series 2 in November 1964, and the bolt-on arrangement, with threaded studs and nuts. For the knock-on type, the hubs and stub-axles were those of the +2, with peg drive. The five pegs per hub were an interference fit and at first they had heads, for which recesses were provided behind the hubs. Later, they were parallel and pressed home with the hubs hot, a stronger construction resulting from the

Interior of a Special Equipment Series 2 Elan with full-width veneered dashboard, locking glove compartment and large-diameter but slim-rimmed steering wheel. The ignition switch on this car is not too conveniently placed to the left of the gear lever.

Rolling chassis of a Series 3 Elan. The extreme rigidity of the steel backbone was fundamental in ensuring that the car achieved the high levels of roadholding and responsiveness which Colin Chapman, as much as his customers, demanded.

omission of the head recesses.

As is well known, knock-on hub caps tend to be self-tightening, but it is extremely important to realize that the Lotus hub caps tighten in the opposite direction to the traditional Rudge type, used for so many years with wire-spoked wheels. The reason is that whereas the Rudge caps fit over the conical hubs of the wheels, the Lotus cones are internal and the caps fit inside them.

The danger is that one might follow the traditional rules and assemble an Elan with the hubs on the wrong sides. The wheels would then be self-loosening instead of self-tightening, the resulting accident being screamingly funny to other people but not to the occupants of the car. So, capitals please Mr. Printer,

hubs with RIGHT-HAND threads on RIGHT-HAND side (coloured green), hubs with LEFT-HAND threads on LEFT-HAND side (coloured red). Also, make sure that the wheel is home on the pegs before belting the cap, as it's just possible that you might push the pegs in flush, which would be another way of having an accident.

The above is not intended to be any sort of criticism of peg-drive wheels, which have some practical advantages over the fine-splined type. Nevertheless, it's something that I always check, ever since I nearly drove off in a road-test car that had its hubs assembled on the wrong sides. Some people don't believe in the self-tightening effect, but just try it the wrong way round, that's all!

The standard tyre size at first was 5.20-13 and then 145-13, but after March 1968 the S4 model had flared wheel-arches and wider tyres could be used if desired. Then 155-13 tyres became a Special Equipment option and finally 155 HR 13 could be regarded as standard — if anything was really standard on a car that could be tailored to suit the owner's whim.

The spare wheel lay flat beneath the left side of the floor of the luggage boot. Naturally one did not expect this compartment to be of family saloon size, but it was of quite reasonable capacity for such a small sports car. Convertible bodies had a well to receive the folding hood, the fabric being separate from the sticks and demanding some effort to stretch into position. Perhaps the word 'convertible' generally implies an American roadster with a top that goes up by pressing a button, but the Elan was not like that!

The battery was behind the passenger's seat on Series 1 Elans, but all subsequent models carried it in the boot. There were various seats, according to fashion and availability, but they were all adjustable fore-and-aft by a slider at the rear and a rocker-type attachment in front. Upholstery was never luxurious and the trim was in an imitation leather, such as vinyl. In a narrow two-seater it is never easy to wind the windows up and down, and thus electrical operation was popular, and was catalogued from the Series 3 in September 1965. The steering column was arranged to telescope as a safety feature and this could be used as an adjustment, by loosening the clamp.

Power house of a Series 3 Elan. With water pump and exhaust manifolding on one side and twin-choke carburettors and substantial air box on the other. The Ford-based Lotus twin-cam engine fills most of the front compartment, but a wide-opening front-hinged lid facilitates top-end maintenance.

The Series 3 convertible in Special Equipment form. The most obvious change from the Series 2 is to framed door windows, which has also brought a subtle change to the line of the leading edge of the doors. Instead of push-pull grips, the windows are now electrically operated.

The car illustrated on the previous page with the hood erected, revealing a commendably neat fit. The waist-height door pull on the far side can just be seen through the driver's door window. The Series 3 convertible had been preceded a few months earlier by the first Lotus Elan coupe.

While the first Elans had a small instrument panel on the driver's side of the car, from Series 2 a full-width wood-veneer facia was adopted, improved and fitted with rocker switches from Series 4. The panel was extended downwards to cover the console, which united the scuttle to the central back-bone — no other open car had such a rigid scuttle as the Elan, in spite of the wide doors.

Standard instruments were speedometer, rev-counter, fuel gauge, and combined water temperature and oil pressure gauges in a single dial. There was sufficient space for those owners who wished to endow their cars with further dials. Small flap-valves for fresh-air ventilation were mounted on the facia and these were surprisingly effective. The heater was of simple construction, but potent and easy to control. When maximum screen

defrosting was desired, the flaps on either side of the heater unit could be closed and the fan turned full on.

The headlamps were retractable, the system operating in one direction by engine vacuum and in the other by a spring. There were, in fact, two distinct systems, the earlier one relying on vacuum to raise the lamps and on the spring to retract them, when the vacuum switch had been moved to admit air to the vacuum cylinder. In this system each headlamp had its own microswitch and automatically switched itself on when approaching the vertical position.

The later system was called 'fail-safe' and the change was made in response to Federal regulations. The operation was completely reversed, the lamps rising under spring pressure and retracting by the pull of the vacuum cylinder. In this case, the microswitch was integral with the vacuum switch and the individual microswitches were deleted. There was a relay in the headlamp circuit, and as the current came via the ignition switch the headlamps would not light unless the ignition was switched on, though they could be raised (by the vacuum in the reservoir or by the spring) and the side lamps would light. Many Elans, including all the earlier ones, had a flasher unit so that the lamps came up flashing until the switch was placed in the 'steady' position.

In order to obtain sufficient reserve vacuum, the front box-section cross-member of the chassis was arranged as an air-tight vessel. This was exhausted by a pipe from the induction system of the engine, with a non-return valve to retain the vacuum when the engine was stopped. This arrangement applied to both types of headlamp operation, although a very few cars originally had separate reservoirs. Incidentally, it is easy to spot those late Elans with the fail-safe system because natural slight leakages allow the headlamps to begin rising after a few hours.

For reasons that have already been explained, few Lotus Elans follow the standard specification exactly and early ones have often been brought up-to-date in several important respects. However, here are a few milestones in the evolution of the Elan, but please regard the dates as approximate.

*   *   *

October 1962, Lotus Elan 1500 presented at Earls Court Motor Show, at £1,095 in kit form or £1,499 complete, including purchase tax.

May 1963, 1558 cc 105 bhp engine replaced 1500 cc unit, which was recalled. Optional hardtop offered.

November 1964, Series 2 introduced. Larger front brake calipers standardized. Centre-lock road wheels optional. Full-width wood-veneer facia with lockable glove box. Smaller pedal pads and quick-release filler cap.

September 1965, Series 3 fixed-head coupé introduced, boot lid extended to the back of the rear deck, and battery mounted in boot. Final drive with 3.55:1 ratio available.

November 1965, close-ratio gearbox optional.

January 1966, Special Equipment model announced with 115

The major change at the rear of Series 3 Elans was the extended luggage compartment lid, which now embraced the lip above the vertical rear panel and enabled the twist lock to be placed above the rear number plate. The retracted radio aerial on one side is balanced by the quick-release fuel filler on the other.

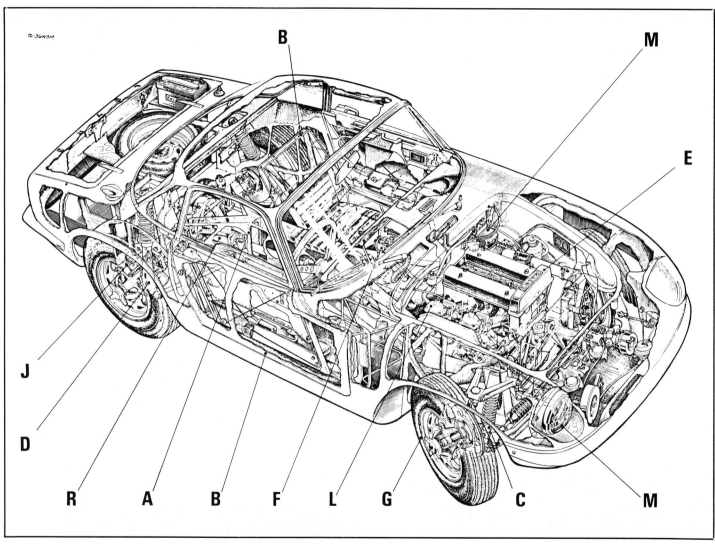

Cutaway drawing of the Series 3 Elan, which was produced at the time of introduction of the coupe for the Lotus workshop manual, hence the ring of identification letters. The manner in which the propeller shaft threads its way through the chassis backbone is shown clearly, as are the two headlamp positions, the right in an operational state, the left retracted.

bhp engine, close-ratio gearbox, servo-assisted brakes, centre-lock wheels and repeater flashers on front wheel-arches.

June 1966, Series 3 convertible introduced with framed door windows, but otherwise similar to fixed-head coupé.

March 1968, Series 4 Elan fixed-head coupé and convertible announced with flared wheel-arches for low-profile tyres, rocker switches on facia, rear lights as on +2, bulge on bonnet and perforated seat trim.

November 1968, two Stromberg carburettors replaced two twin-choke Webers on cylinder-heads with siamesed inlet ports.

August 1969, return of Weber carburettors (or Dellortos) and eight-port heads.

February 1971, Elan S4 Sprint introduced with Tony Rudd's big-valve 126 bhp engine, strengthened differential and drive-shafts and stronger drive-shaft couplings. Body finished in two-colour scheme.

Alternate Elans. The introduction of a fixed-head coupe version of the Elan in the autumn of 1965 was in line with the growing interest in the Grand Touring type of car as an alternative to the open sports car. In Series 3 form the two Elans were being offered with a higher level of equipment and refinement than hitherto.

An Elan coupe in component form. For anyone with adequate garage space, some lifting tackle, a reasonable level of mechanical aptitude and a good tool kit the task of final assembly was not too onerous. Note the ventilation grilles behind the door windows, which were added during the life of the Series 3 coupe.

There were numerous changes of badging during the production life of the Elan, one example being on the Series 3 coupe, where some cars carried 'Coupe S/E' on the body sides, as this example, while others were badged 'Elan Coupe S/E'. Although UK-registered, this car is a left-hand-drive model.

August 1973, Elan production discontinued.

* * *

The price of the Elan no doubt varied somewhat, according to the arrangements made for the supply of the parts. In 1964 its basic price was £1,187, or £1,436 with purchase tax. Probably the cost in component form did not suffer greatly from the former figure. By 1970 the amounts had risen to £1,595 and £2,084 respectively, but although over £2,000 was a high price for a small car in those days, hardly anybody actually paid purchase tax, it would appear.

This supposition is reinforced by a change of policy that took place in 1971. At that time, the Elan Sprint, with Tony Rudd's big-valve engine, could only be bought in component form, the price quoted being £1,663. No doubt a completely legal and watertight system for the supply of components had by then been worked out, so as to avoid the ban on the marketing of complete tax-free kits. Before that date, the purchase had tended to be rather an under-the-counter transaction.

Whereas the Elan could only be bought in DIY form, the up-market Plus 2S 130 would soon be available solely as a complete car, with purchase tax paid. There is no reason whatever to denigrate the Elan because it was an assembled job. The process of building it up was remarkably easy, and most of the amateur assemblers regarded it as a labour of love. Furthermore, they could afford to spend far more time, at every stage, than could be spared commercially.

Before a Lotus warranty would be issued, the car had to be taken along to the dealer for a searching mechanical scrutiny. This was desirable in the interest of road safety, as well as to protect the good name of the manufacturers. Reassured by this compulsory check, the insurance companies raised no objection to the last stages of the assembly taking place away from the parent factory.

The above refers to the assembly of road-going Elans. The process of building Elans for racing was an entirely different proposition and this, along with development and preparation, will be covered in a later chapter.

Much of the attraction of the Elan came from its very compact dimensions; with a wheelbase of 7 ft, a front track of 3 ft 11 in and a rear track of 4 ft (plus or minus a fraction according to wheel and tyre equipment), the Elan was really a small car. This allowed the width to be kept down to 4 ft 8 in, which was marvellous for the rapid negotiation of traffic, and the overall length of 12 ft 1 in saved a lot of money when shipping the car abroad.

The Elan was sturdily constructed and the body was far from fragile, except when lightened for racing. The use of many standard components from the big manufacturers made weight-saving difficult, but clever design and, above all, small overall dimensions, made it possible to keep the weight down to just over 14 cwt. So many cars grow steadily heavier over the years, but the Elan never did. On the other hand, the twin-cam engine started with 105 bhp, went up to 115 bhp, and finally, in

Metal kick plates were a sensible provision on the lower front corners of the door trim, as were the cutaway panels to provide an important small increase in elbow room in a rather compact cockpit.

Cockpit of the Series 3 Elan showing the later type of perforated-spoke steering wheel. On some cars the ignition switch beneath the ashtray was blanked off and placed just below the padded bottom edge of the dashboard behind the steering wheel.

An interesting overhead view of an Elan Series 3 Special Equipment coupe revealing the smooth contours of what has proved to be a timeless design. The cylindrical items forward of the rear parcel shelf are the reels for the safety belts.

The fourth stage in the evolution of the Elan came in March 1968 with the introduction of the S4 convertible and coupe. Amongst the changes were flared wheel arches to accommodate the wider tyres which were part of the Special Equipment package and later were to be adopted across the S4 range.

Another change of badging produced the 'ELAN' name behind the front wheel and an 'SE' symbol on the rear quarter panel of Special Equipment models.

Substantial interior changes on the S4 Elan included the use of rocker controls on the dashboard, the addition of small ventilation flaps in the corners, and completely changed door trim incorporating recessed release handles and locks and ventilated covering to match the revised seat trim.

The main identification feature of a Series 4 Elan compared with the Series 3 is the use of larger rear-light clusters, as fitted to the Plus 2, on the newer model. This example also has a twin-outlet exhaust system.

This side view of a Series 4 coupe shows very clearly the flatter line of the extended wheel arches, also the power bulge in the engine cover, which was another S4 identification feature. Note yet another variation in the use of badges.

big-valve form, gave a rousing 126 bhp.

A 126 bhp engine in a car weighing only 14 cwt adds up to a performance which, even now, is outstanding. In its day, the Elan could out-perform anything on the road, except costly cars with far larger engines.

The ultimate maximum speed was always limited by the relatively low gearing. The engine was normally equipped with a governor on the ignition, which cut out at about 6,600 rpm. This was generally removed from Press cars and some highly immoral revolutions were attained, but most private owners were less inclined to risk their engines, while their warranty would be invalidated if they were caught without a rev-limiter.

There were three final-drive ratios, 3.90, which was standard on the earliest cars, 3.77 and 3.55:1. Cars of the first series had a timed maximum speed of 114 or 115 mph, which fell to 108 mph with the ignition cut-out in place. The best timed speed recorded in a road test was 124 mph, with the 3.55:1 final-drive and 155 HR 13 tyres, which entailed holding an engine speed of 7,130 rpm. The best speed recorded with a cut-out installed was 121 mph by a Sprint, so one assumes that the cut-out was one of those lucky ones that allowed 6,800 rpm or so, instead of the usual 6,600 rpm.

Two views of a 'Federalized' Series 4 coupe, the changes to which include the use of spanner-tightened wheel nuts in place of the three-eared knock-on type, front and rear repeater lights on the body sides and a large rear-view mirror on the driver's door. By this time the ventilation grilles were recessed neatly within a moulded lip.

Rindt in a Sprint. Although the Elan S4 Sprint was not catalogued until early in 1971, several months after the tragic death of Jochen Rindt at Monza, a prototype was produced in 1970 and taken to Brands Hatch for publicity photographs with the Lotus Grand Prix team-leader. A different two-tone colour scheme was adopted for the production version.

I have not yet been able to get my hands on one of the very few five-speed Elans, but a Sprint so equipped should be good for something approaching 130 mph. Of course the racing version, the Lotus 26R, with its steel crankshaft and 140 bhp, was a different proposition altogether.

An analysis of all the contemporary road-test reports shows a spectacular improvement over the years in acceleration, apart from a slight pause during the period of the Zenith-Stromberg carburettors. A 0–60 mph figure of 8.7 seconds was typical in 1964, with 7.6s in 1967 and 7.3s in 1970. Finally, the Sprint recorded 6.7s in 1971. For uniformity, I have quoted *Motor* and *Autocar* figures, which were taken with two men in the car. Lotus themselves claimed 0–60 mph in 6.2s, but this was presumably with only the driver aboard.

Fuel-consumption figures were invariably excellent, 30 mpg

An interesting variation in windscreen wiper arrangements. As was usual practice, the Bell & Colvill demonstrator has the wipers parked to the driver's side whereas the convertible with the hood erected has the wipers parked to the left, even though the steering wheel is on the right.

being typical even when the cars were driven really hard, though the more powerful Sprint was naturally rather thirstier. Larger-engined cars could equal the performance of the Elan, but always at the cost of a far heavier petrol consumption.

It is interesting to read the contemporary road test reports which were published during the car's production. Without exception, the testers were impressed by the remarkably comfortable ride, for very hard springing was still considered quite acceptable among small sports cars. The roadholding and handling seemed to come as a great surprise to some of these writers, who evidently associated comfort with sloppy cornering, and many superlatives were applied to the behaviour on winding roads.

The controllability was greatly assisted by the high-geared

An attractive-looking two-tone Sprint coupe with the model name let into a narrow band in a third colour at approximately bumper height. The long badge between the front wheel arch and the driver's door celebrates the Lotus victories in the World Championship since 1963.

This is the interior of the immaculate Big Valve-engined Elan S4 illustrated on the jacket of this book and owned by David Everard. The pull switch just to the left of the lower steering-wheel spoke is for raising and lowering the headlamps, while the positioning of the ignition switch to the right of the steering column is one of several clues that this is one of the later-model Elans.

and accurate steering, with 2½ turns of the wheel from lock to lock. However, most of the testers criticized the roadholding on wet roads. Quite why this should be is difficult to fathom for, as a general rule, softly sprung cars tend to behave well on slippery surfaces. Perhaps some of these drivers were unaccustomed to light cars with a lot of power, but it is more likely that the tyres of that era were to blame. There has been a veritable revolution in tread design and rubber mixes during the last few years, and it seems likely that this criticism would not have been made if modern tyres had been available.

The test-drivers were unanimous in hating the winding and unwinding of the doughnut rubbers on the drive-shafts. When at last the redesigned Rotoflex joints were substituted there was a general sigh of relief; it is astonishing that it took so long for this universal dissatisfaction to be heeded. Another grumble was that the retractable headlights were not really powerful enough for the speed potential of the car, and extra spotlights, legal and otherwise, were often fitted by owners.

Throughout the years of production, there was a moan about gear ratios, and in particular concerning excessive revs at cruising speeds. On Continental motorways, speeds as high as 100 mph were frequently maintained, and this became tiring because of the engine noise. However, the 3.55:1 ratio for the final-drive was the 'longest' that was available and anything like 3.0:1 would in any case have made bottom gear too high for rapid getaways or restarting on steep hills. As previously mentioned, a few 'unofficial' five-speed Elans were built right at the end of production, and that would have been the perfect answer.

The final moan concerned accessibility, and certainly the distributor and fuel pump were well buried. The DIY man did not mind a little extra work, and the flexibly mounted carburettors could soon be taken off, but the garage bill for merely fitting new points might seem out of proportion.

The high standard of body construction and the promise of freedom from rust earned universal approval. The vivid acceleration, assisted by the excellent traction afforded by the inde-

pendent rear suspension, also inspired great enthusiasm. Nevertheless, it was the roadholding and, above all, the handling that caused normally unemotional journalists to wax poetic.

As the road-test driver for *Autosport*, I drove Elans regularly throughout their currency. I remember many epic journeys to such places as Le Mans and the Frankfurt Motor Show, the latter trip including some enjoyable races with 911 Porsches, but also a very nasty spot of bother with the German police!

Yet, I distrust reminiscences and most of all my own! It's so easy to look at the past through rose-coloured glasses and so I decided that it was essential to borrow — if I could — a representative example and put it through its paces. Cars are getting better all the time, so they say, and I wondered how it would compare with the modern exotica which I drive for a living (poor chap!).

That was easier said than done until I mentioned my dilemma to Ian Webb. He put me in touch with those great Lotus enthusiasts, Bobby Bell and Martin Colvill, who insisted that

The Lotus twin-cam engine was seen in its most powerful production-car form in the Elan with the announcement of the Sprint model in 1971. With the aid of Tony Rudd's Big Valve cylinder-head maximum power was increased to 126 bhp. Here we see both the European installation, which featured Weber carburettors apart from a short spell with Dellortos, and the American-market set-up, with twin Strombergs and crossover pipes from the exhaust side. This American installation also has a cover plate over the spark plug well.

An American-market Elan Sprint with Federal-type wheel nuts, another design of name badge and one headlamp visible in the raised position.

there was no problem, as the French say. At the drop of a hat, my deerstalker actually, they produced a customer who not only owned an Elan in mint condition but was willing to let me borrow it. This brave fellow, David Everard, has my eternal gratitude.

Perhaps one had almost forgotten how tiny this Lotus is. It was so narrow that the door touched my right arm, discouraging the flailing elbows of my hill-climb days. Yet it was almost a luxury car in miniature, with electrically-operated windows, excellent heating and ventilation, and a comfortable ride. The wide doors made entry surprisingly easy, a far cry indeed from the tough, doorless Seven.

On moving off, I was surprised to find how flexible the engine was, accepting top gear at quite a low speed and fairly romping up hills on that ratio. However, the excellent gearbox was meant to be used and I soon found that all the old magic was there. The car accelerated strongly on any gear, but it was best to let the willing engine have its head, changing up just as the rev-limiter was about to come into play.

The small size is a potent safety factor, for one can always squeeze through narrowing gaps and it's almost like riding a good motorcycle through traffic. The wide cars of today never give an impression of speed, but in the little Elan I recaptured the feeling of excitement as the speedometer swung past the 100-mph mark. The road seemed to be rushing towards me, rather as it used to in the Type 35 Bugatti, and curves were taken by a mere flexing of the wrists, thanks to the high-geared steering.

Approaching what looked quite a steep hill at low speed, I ran up through the gears, the car accelerating as if it was on the level and going over the crest at over 100 mph — that's what low weight and a small frontal area can do. I had to remind myself repeatedly that the engine was of only 1600 cc, for on winding roads there are few cars indeed that could keep up with an Elan, even now.

There are quieter cars, especially at really high cruising speeds, but it was the right sort of sound and not at all tiring. Earlier Elans had a rather insistent exhaust note, but David Everard's car has the later silencer, which avoids unwelcome attention from you-know-whom. It also has the stronger doughnut couplings and I never noticed any winding-and-unwinding effects.

In a few words, a really good Lotus Elan is more fun to drive than any car (except perhaps the Super Seven, when it isn't raining!) that is made today, while its performance is still outstanding.

To conclude this rather long chapter, here is a note for those who collect Lotus numbers. The original Elan was the Lotus 26 and the competition version was the 26R. The fixed-head coupé was the 36 and the S3 drophead coupé was the 45. Production continued for well over ten years and 7,895 of Series 1 to 3 were sold, followed by 2,976 of the S4 and 1,353 of the Sprint. The grand total was 12,224, so quite a lot of motoring enthusiasts were able to learn what fun driving could be.

My friend Jabby Crombac, who edits *Sport-Auto* in Paris and drives enormous distances to races, has for many years used Elans as his personal transport. Let us give him a chapter to himself, to describe his experiences in his own words.

CHAPTER 4

My Elans

by Gérard (Jabby) Crombac

During the course of 14 years I have owned two Lotus Elans. The first one was in daily use and this was the case of the second one for about five years. It is now part of my collection, but still used constantly. It is spared the hassle of the Paris traffic (and especially the parking chore which ends up in constantly scratched nose paint) but used whenever I drive alone to a race meeting.

My first Elan was an S2 drophead which was delivered new in 1965. Its first few months were not without problems, but when everything was put right (including changing the starter motor ring on the flywheel, which was of the wrong pitch) I had some wonderful times with it. After two years, however, I found the car, despite very careful maintenance, aged very badly. This was especially the case with the running gear and hubs, and the steering rack developed a tremendous amount of play. Apart from this, the main trouble I had with this car was a constant and never cured tendency to overheat in traffic.

During the winter of '66–67, Jimmy Clark wrote to me from Tasmania, offering to share a flat in Paris with me, as he had taken up residence in Bermuda and needed a European base. When he got settled in the Spring he collected his company car, a brand new left-hand-drive yellow S/E coupé. The difference between this car and my own S2 — only two years older — was truly fantastic; no more overheating, much more silent running, better heating and ventilation, and a tremendous improvement in the finish. Jimmy also had his plane, a twin Comanche Piper, available in Paris, but he grew so fond of his Elan that unless he was pushed for time he would invariably choose the Elan over

the airplane to go to race meetings.

The Elan is not a tremendously fast car, it would not reach the magic 200 km/h (125 mph), but I am afraid I have to record that whatever top speed it would do, Jimmy would often reach it in the most improbable places. Alan Mann probably remembers to this day when he came to Paris to propose a deal to Jimmy about driving his Ford sports car. He had made a mistake in the time of his departure and when he checked his ticket there was only about three-quarters of an hour to the take-off. They were still in our flat in the middle of Paris, and Alan was departing from Le Bourget, due north. He made it! Jimmy never had any serious problems except with the radio, linked to a stereo tape recorder, which he could never get to work properly.

During the winter the car was garaged in the basement and when Jimmy came back he was through his period of one year, during which he could not get back to England (he had obtained a special permission for the British GP), and at last he was going to be able to return to visit his family and see his farm at Duns. He had arranged with Lotus to pick up a new company car and this was going to be a +2, the latest model which Colin Chapman insisted that he should be seen in, in order to promote its sale. I had made a deal with Lotus to take over the S/E Coupé when Jimmy would not need it any more. My S2, however, was getting very, very tired, as I mentioned earlier, and very kindly, although his 2 + 2 wasn't ready yet, Jimmy agreed to let me take over the S/E immediately as he wasn't going to be in Paris for a while anyway. So in April '68, as he was to fly over to Hockenheim to take part in a Formula 2 race, it was agreed that

No, this picture did not creep into a book about Lotus by mistake. It was taken at Silverstone in the summer of 1979, when author John Bolster was reunited with the ERA which he drove in the 1949 British Grand Prix, when he suffered a very serious accident which terminated his racing career. Jabby Crombac seems to find the famous ERA rather amusing, the irrepressible Elan enthusiast doubtless believing any car without a backbone chassis to be automatically suspect. Unfortunately his ex-Jim Clark Elan was undergoing renovation at the time this book was being prepared, and consequently could not be illustrated in this chapter.

I would go with him to Toussus le Noble airport, where he kept the Comanche. Upon arrival, he handed the keys of the car over to me: 'This is your car now' he said, and he took off. I never saw him again as he was killed in that race.

This is how NLD 550E became by cherished possession, 11 years ago.

The car was obviously in very good shape, but when I drove it to the Dutch GP that year it was raining, and I found the engine missing quite badly at high revs. Also, that radio still wasn't working properly. I had taken the car to a specialist in Paris who said, 'I know these cars, a good customer of mine has one, we could never get the radio to work properly, the fault is with this damn glass-fibre!' I even lined the bonnet with metallic gauze to make a Faraday cage, all to no avail. He had mentioned the

name of this customer. When the dynamo went for the first time (there were many more . . .) the electrician had noticed the radio suppressor on the coil was connected the wrong way. 'Your ignition must have been upset and also the radio' he said. True enough, this cured all my problems.

Soon afterwards I happed to meet the owner of this other Elan in which the radio also didn't work, and true enough the suppressor was fitted the wrong way round . . . I suppose the same bloke had put our cars together at the factory! In 11 years, I have seen the speedo recorder go round the clock once and the car has now reached 126,000 km (78,300 miles). It has never let me down.

The troubles I had were mainly the electrics (several dynamos and starter-motor rebuilds and once a window electrical wind-up mechanism). The rev-counter never works accurately for more than six months, after which it becomes 500 rpm fast, so I stopped changing it.

I twice had trouble with the gearbox; an oil leak made it overheat the first time and the second time we found one of the synchro rings had been reinserted the wrong way round (it took several years to make itself felt!). Perhaps the worst was a chassis fracture close to the gearbox stay. It was possible to weld it up *in situ*, but to anybody buying a secondhand Elan I would suggest a check there. I am also through my second crownwheel-and-pinion.

Engine-wise, I had three difficult moments. One was a broken water pump, the second when the piston rings wore out and the plugs were getting oiled up. This was especially the case when running in traffic, of course, and until we attended to it I had to carry a bottle of acetone to clean the plugs. The third one was very peculiar; one jet got blocked in one carburettor, which made for erratic running on one cylinder. I was, however, unable to detect this as I had found out an engine stay was broken (I understand this is another frequent cause of trouble). I nursed the car back to Paris from the French GP, but when we had substituted a new engine stay it was found that the engine was running on three cylinders; 300 miles with the blocked jet had overheated the starved cylinder to the extent that one valve was burned.

Early on the camshaft cover gasket used to leak frequently, as the sump ventilation is a little insufficient, which would pressurize it. We have put in an extra breather, which cured this problem, and also modified the throttle cable actuation of the carburettors.

I went through a couple of exhaust systems and when the first one went I didn't change it soon enough. Hot gases were leaking on to the clutch hydraulic system plastic pipe, which was burned, so I brought the car back from one GP clutchless (it restarted all right in bottom on the starter motor when I had to stop in traffic).

A few years ago, while in London, the car was stolen in front of the hotel at Victoria Station. Imagine my fears! The police inspector told me: 'They probably nicked it to put the engine into an Escort, you will find the bare shell in a few weeks' time!' But the thief didn't go far; a few minutes after he had stolen it he lost it in a corner and ended up on the pavement, with two buckled wheels and a bent front upright. No sooner had I got back to Paris than John Bolster — whose address I had given to the police — rang me up to bring the good news. All this was quickly repaired, but the trouble is with the wheels, which haven't been properly straightened up. I checked with Lotus and they said that this type of wheel (knock-off) is like gold dust. For the time being, I have to put up with exaggerated tyre wear . . .

In 1970, during the shooting of the film 'Le Mans', in which I was a technical adviser, I did the return trip Paris–Le Mans daily (300 miles) for several days until one morning at 5 am, when I wasn't fully awake, I crashed into the back of an ambulance. This is the only body damage it has ever suffered (right front corner). The car was entirely repainted when I decided not to use it daily any more and spare it the Paris traffic.

One thing I was never able to get to stay in place is the alloy strip between the bumper and nose. Also, the ventilation well at the base of the windscreen has drain holes which are too small and clog up. As a result, each time you have had the car washed, when you take the first corner water comes down on your feet, cascading from the heater outlet . . . I have had the opportunity to drive the later models from Lotus, but one thing I really enjoy in the Elan (and also in my Super Seven) is its small size and especially its narrowness. I know the Elan could not be sold in Sweden as it did not pass the local rules over body width, but to me this is precisely an advantage. I wish I could put an Esprit or an Eclat next to it in my garage, but I certainly will never part with my Elan. I hope my son Colin-James will feel the same way about it . . .

CHAPTER 5

The Plus 2

The family man's Elan

Originally named the Elan +2, the larger model, which survived the Elan, was later called simply +2 or Plus 2. Introduced in June 1967, it was of similar design and construction to the Elan, but a foot longer in the wheelbase and seven inches wider in the track, while the overall length was stretched by just an inch under a couple of feet. Naturally, this much bigger car was heavier, the extra weight amounting to rather over 3 cwt.

The primary object of the +2 was to contain a pair of small extra seats. These were intended for children up to early teenage size, but adults could use them for short journeys if the front seats were moved forward. The greater width gave an altogether more spacious interior, the driver enjoying plenty of elbow room, which tended to be cramped in the Elan. The +2 had a remarkably low drag coefficient and many people preferred its appearance to that of the smaller car.

Although this was a much more substantial vehicle, the 1558 cc twin-cam engine was employed to propel it. This was in a high state of tune, developing 118 bhp, and during the period when the Elan went over to Zenith Stromberg carburettors the +2 retained its twin-choke Webers, except on those cars with Federal emission equipment. A brake servo was standard and the body had through-flow ventilation. The transmission resembled that of the Elan, as previously described, with the 3.77:1 final-drive ratio. The propeller shaft and drive-shafts were longer, of course, and that goes for the suspension and steering links, too.

The chassis frame, welded up from steel pressings, was a similar backbone to that of the Elan with suitably enlarged dimensions; the box-section front cross-member again doubled as a vacuum reservoir for the retractable headlamps. Some large holes were pierced in the sheet steel, both for lightness and for accessibility at strategic points.

In shape, the chassis was a rectangular central girder spreading out into forks at either end, to which cross-members were welded to carry the suspension. The earliest frames were found to have a weakness at the rear, due to inadequate welding. Lotus dealers were instructed how to re-weld the sharp corners in the form of a fillet, which overcame the trouble permanently.

Beneath the rear cross-member, the differential unit was suspended by the arms of the light-alloy casing, which were bolted up against rubber mountings. It was located in a fore-and-aft direction by lower torque rods attached to the main chassis member. Again, there was a problem here in early cars, for the arms of the casing occasionally broke (it happened to me!). This was partly due to the increased torque of the tuned engine, but principally to the greater weight of the new car, which prevented wheelspin as a safety valve. The solution was a thicker casting.

The +2 was the first Lotus to have a brake servo as standard. In the case of cars intended for certain markets, dual hydraulic circuits were used, with a tandem master-cylinder; in this instance, two separate servo units were employed. The +2 had the brake discs mounted on the inner sides of the rear bearing housings, as described in the Elan chapter. However, the +2 differed in having dirt shields over the brakes, which were fitted after the first few cars. Some owners removed these shields

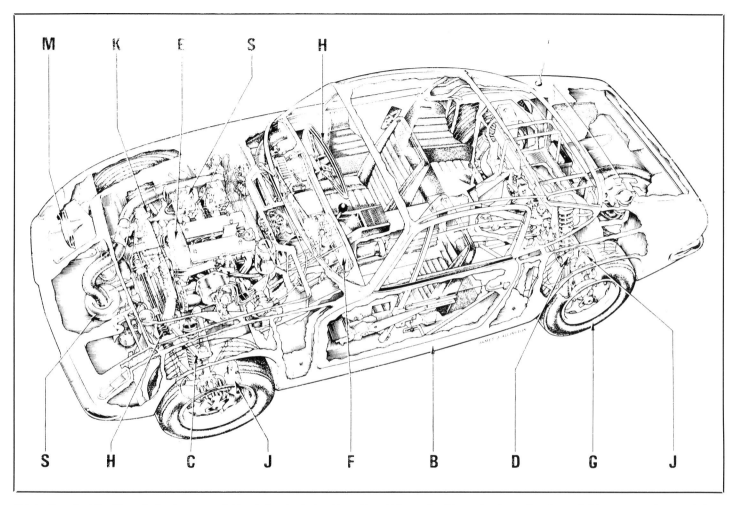

Originally called the Elan+2, the larger model is obviously derived from the old favourite. A two-plus-two rather than a full four-seater, it nevertheless provides ample space for two lucky children, while the driver and front passenger have plenty of elbow room. Powered by the famous Lotus twin-cam engine, the larger car is not far behind the Elan in performance, especially the later 130S version, which has the Big Valve unit developing 126 bhp. This is a James Allington cutaway from the Lotus workshop manual.

A significantly larger luggage compartment is one of the advantages of the Plus 2 over the two-seater Elan. The 'ELAN+2' badge to the right of the rear number plate identifies this as one of the earlier examples.

because they obstructed the examination and replacement of the outer Rotoflex joints.

Most cars have now been fitted with the later exhaust system, but as this is meant to be a serious historical work, let's begin at the beginning. At first the +2 had a cast-iron manifold, properly arranged with paired pipes for extractor action, which was bolted to side-by-side downpipes that merged into one after the bottom bend. Thereafter, an intermediate pipe carried the gases to a transverse silencer at the rear, with a heat shield above it to avoid boiling the beer, if crates were carried in the boot.

Later cars had a deeper boot and there was no longer sufficient space for a transverse silencer. The new component was mounted fore-and-aft, again with a heat shield above it, and the intermediate pipe was of a different shape to accommodate this. A new fabricated manifold became available, which was integral with the downpipes, and curiously enough it proved to be quieter than the earlier pattern, although cast-iron is usually regarded as the best noise absorber. There was also a cast-iron

The luggage compartment lid raised to reveal the simple but effective supporting arrangement. The extra width of the Plus 2 body over that of the Elan two-seaters was a major factor in providing adequate luggage space, although during the course of the production life of the larger car further modifications were made at the rear to increase the depth of the compartment.

The same car revealing a more elaborate dashboard than on the two-seater Elan and full-depth door trim without the need for elbow cutaways.

As on the Elan the retractable headlamps offer a low and smoothly contoured body line at the front, but the larger body has the side and indicator lights above instead of beneath the front bumper blade.

Brand Lotus '10-spoke' wheels give the Plus 2S a distinctive appearance. The filler cap is on the left side on this model, hence the mounting of the radio aerial on the right.

Although there is an unmistakable family resemblance, the detail body design of the Elan coupe and the Plus 2 have little in common. Note in particular the different treatment of the door opening below the front screen pillar.

manifold, incorporating the necessary heating chamber, for the crossover pipes of Federal emission engines.

The body was of glass-fibre, laminated and finished in the same way as that of the Elan, previously described. It had similar steel reinforcement, particularly round the door apertures. The general thickness of the panels was $\frac{1}{8}$ in (3.17 mm), increasing to $\frac{1}{4}$ in (6.35 mm) in highly stressed regions, such as seat mountings, floor areas and wheel-arch lips. The front seats were differently mounted from those of the Elan, having orthodox slides and tipping forward for access to the rear compartment.

In October 1968 the +2S was introduced, though the +2 remained in production for a while. The +2S broke entirely new ground, for it was the first Lotus that could not be bought in kit form; it was sold completely assembled and full purchase tax had to be paid. The interior was altogether more luxuriously

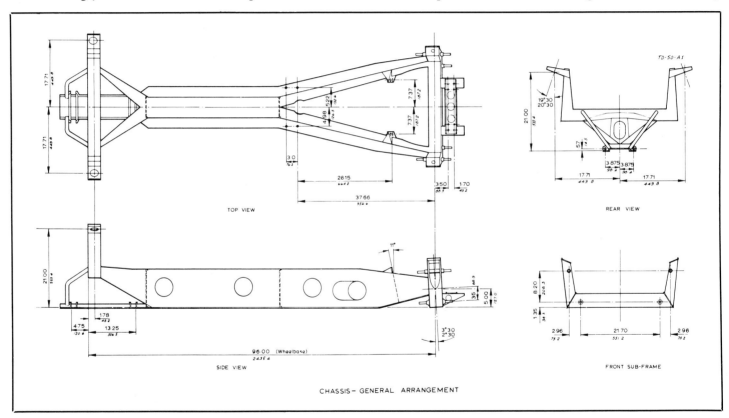

CHASSIS – GENERAL ARRANGEMENT

The chassis of the Plus 2 is an enlarged version of the Elan backbone and has the glass-fibre body fitted over it like a saddle. Ahead of the front cross-member there is provision for mounting the steering rack, and at the rear the backbone has a lower extension to provide anchorage points for the wide-based wishbones.

furnished and there was extra equipment, such as fog lights. It was at about this time that an alternator replaced the DC generator.

In December 1969 the ordinary +2 was discontinued, but the +2S was selling well to a rather different type of customer from previous Lotus models. It was the first sign that Colin Chapman intended to go up-market. In February 1971, the +2S was replaced in its turn by the +2S 130. This had the 126 bhp big-valve engine of the Elan Sprint and could be identified by its silver roof. While all previous Lotus bodies had undergone an orthodox spray-painting routine, the silver roof of the +2S 130 was self-coloured.

The final metamorphosis of the +2 series was in October 1972, when a five-speed gearbox became optional. When so fitted, the car was called +2S 130/5, a mystic sign that was emblazoned on the left rear quarter of the body. This was the

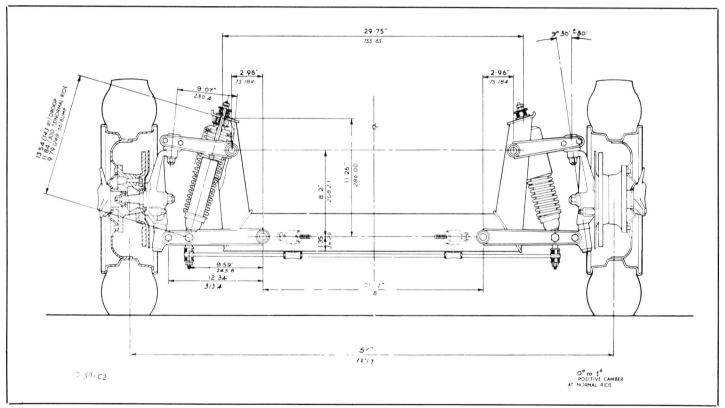

The front suspension is by unequal-length wishbones, with ball-joints at the top of the uprights and trunnions below. The front cross-member has vertical extensions at its outer ends to provide the top mountings for the spring-damper units. The anti-roll bar is carried beneath the cross-member and shares the lower pivot points of the spring-damper units.

improvement which all Lotus models had needed, for it had a direct drive on fourth gear and the final-drive ratio was unchanged. This gave the car the same maximum speed on fourth as it had previously possessed on top, and on the over-drive fifth ratio of 0.80:1 it could achieve about the same speed at 1,400 rpm less, or even go a little faster under favourable conditions.

The strut-type rear suspension of the Plus 2, with lower wide-based wishbones, is identical in principle to that of the Elan except for the wider track. This drawing shows how the hypoid unit is suspended from the rear cross-member, and also illustrates the arrangement of the drive-shafts, with doughnut universal joints at both ends. Knock-on hub spinners are used, with peg-drive wheels.

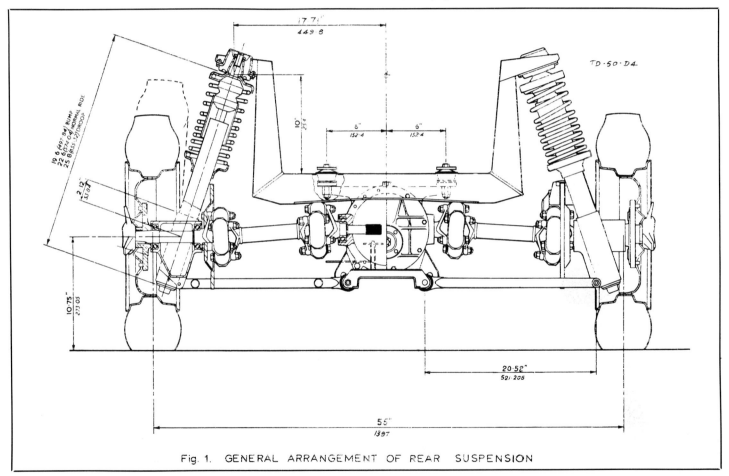

Fig. 1. GENERAL ARRANGEMENT OF REAR SUSPENSION

Thus, the +2S 130/5 had the easy high-speed cruising which other Lotus cars had always lacked. The acceleration was unchanged, for third and second had similar ratios to those of the four-speed box, while first was fractionally lower. The gearbox ratios were 0.80, 1.0, 1.37, 2.0 and 3.20:1. The factor of safety was unusually high, for this was the preliminary version of the gearbox that was to be used later, with the 2-litre 16-valve engine, in the future Elite and Eclat.

At first, the five-speed gearbox had a very heavy change and the operation was far from precise. This was quickly remedied by giving the lever more mechanical advantage, and the box became a pleasure to use. Obviously, it should last for ever when transmitting the power of the 1558 cc twin-cam engine, so the owners of +2S 130/5s, or of those four or five Elan Sprint/5s, are on to a good thing.

Some people thought that the +2 would prove to be under-powered, but that was far from being the case. The maximum speed was similar to that of the Elan, indeed better than that of the earlier cars with less highly tuned engines. The greatest surprise was the acceleration, which suffered remarkably little from the quite considerable increase in weight. This can only have been the result of all that work in the wind tunnel, for plainly the +2 had superior aerodynamics to the Elan.

As for the handling, this was, if anything, even better, too. The Elan, for all its splendid reputation as a roadholder, had just about the minimum wheel track with which good handling can be obtained. This was proved when it was adapted for racing with more powerful engines, as it then became a very tricky little car to drive. Its small dimensions, particularly its narrow overall width, were an immense advantage on winding roads, but the

More equipment and more refinement. This interior is immediately recognizable as that of one of the Plus 2S models by reason of the two additional instruments in the centre section of the dashboard. Notice that compared with the original Plus 2 the lever-type door handles have been replaced by recessed releases and the ashtray has been moved upwards.

An early Elan Plus 2 interior revealing a reasonable amount of space for two children, even though the almost vertical backrest encouraged a rather upright seating position.

wider track of the +2 made it an easier car to handle for the average driver. This is not to belittle the Elan in any way, for its light weight and small size made it an incomparable sports car under most road conditions.

Thumbing through the road tests of *Motor* and *Autocar*, we find the first report on the +2 in 1967, showing a one-way maximum of 125 mph and a mean of three MIRA straights at 122.5 mph. The +2S 130, tested by both magazines, and the +2S 130/5 all recorded an identical 121 mph mean, which was presumably reduced by the tyre scrubbing on the MIRA bankings. Acceleration from a standstill to 60 mph was 8.2 seconds for the earlier car and 7.7, 7.5 and 7.4 second for the later ones.

As for the handling, these test-drivers became all starry-eyed; here's an example. 'The uncanny cornering powers of this remarkable machine equal and probably exceed those of any production car we have driven before; similarly the handling and brakes are certainly not bettered.' Or here's another one. 'Straight away one revels in steering which is high-geared yet so light that you can throw it round even the sharpest corners at very high g without straining at the wheel.'

These writers were also impressed with the riding comfort and they were pleased with the finish of the cars. Apart from small niggles, the only serious complaint once again concerned the retractable headlamps, which lacked power for fast driving at night, though there was a suggestion that the stability in side winds might be better, too.

I tested all the versions of the Lotus +2 for *Autosport*, but memory can play tricks. So, I hied me to my friends, Bobby Bell and Martin Colvill, who had a very clean +2S 130 in stock. Though bigger than an Elan, this is still a compact car, but the interior is considerably more spacious.

I had almost forgotten what a splendid car this is. The light,

The auxiliary lights of this Plus 2S nestle neatly into spaces below the front bumper and each side of the radiator opening, which in turn provides a mounting point for the front number plate.

A Plus 2S in Federal form with standard wheels equipped with non-eared hub caps, semi-recessed front and rear side repeater lights and a driver's door mirror. Neat covers are a useful addition to the low-mounted auxiliary lights.

Finishing touches being applied to Plus 2 bodies prior to trimming at the Lotus assembly plant at Hethel, Norfolk. Body panel thickness ranged from eighth-inch to quarter-inch in more highly stressed areas.

A Plus 2 with headlamps raised. This is one of the earlier cars without the power bulge in the engine compartment lid which appeared in 1969 with the Plus 2S.

The introduction of Tony Rudd's Big Valve version of the Lotus twin-cam engine brought with it the announcement of the Plus 2S 130, a model which was easily distinguishable by a self-coloured silver upper part of the body.

Three-quarter rear view of the Plus 2S 130. This car has the later arrangement of a fore-and-aft exhaust silencer in place of the previous transverse type, the change being in order to accommodate a deeper luggage trunk.

quick steering conveys every message from the road surface to the driver's hands. Somehow, the machine immediately gives one confidence and one rushes into corners without the slightest misgiving. It's so beautifully balanced and the ride is so comfortable — even today there are very few cars that can compare with it. The engine develops a great deal of power for its size, yet it is remarkably flexible and has no objection if one drives lazily.

Earlier Lotus cars tended to have ear-splitting exhaust notes, but this one had the later silencing arrangements and it was actually very quiet. The rear seats were really for children, but small adults might manage and certainly they would have suited my dogs admirably. Admittedly the original +2 had certain weaknesses, but these were all ironed-out and a well-serviced example should still be a perfectly reliable car.

As for the dimensions, the wheelbase was 8 ft, the track 4 ft 6 in (front) and 4 ft 7 in (rear), the overall length was 14 ft and the width 5 ft 3.5 in. The weight, with water, oil and some petrol aboard, was 16.8 cwt for the original +2 and 17.5 cwt for the more elaborately equipped +2S 130/5.

In 1974, a certain amount of redesigning and expensive crash-testing was becoming due, in view of the strict legislation on type approval. As it was Lotus policy to concentrate on the new models with the 2-litre 16-valve engine, the excellent +2 was phased-out, though a few crafty ones appear to have slipped through the net in 1975. Altogether, 3,300 cars were made before production came to an end.

For those who objected to a two-colour Plus 2S 130 the answer was an all-silver car, a paint finish which many people thought displayed the undeniably attractive lines of the two-plus-two body to their maximum advantage, especially when set against darker-colour wheels.

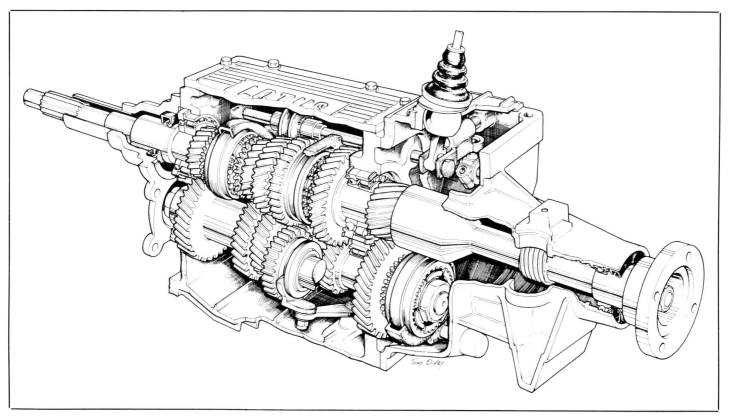

A highly popular refinement towards the end of the Plus 2S lifespan was the introduction of a five-speed gearbox, which did wonders for the cars high-speed cruising ability. Early examples had a heavy change, but this problem was quickly overcome. The new gearbox led to the model designation Plus 2S 130/5, a rather ponderous name for an outstanding car. The last few Elans were also equipped with the five-speed transmission.

CHAPTER 6

The Renault engine and transmission

Introducing an international element

Many people were surprised when, in 1966, Colin Chapman produced a new mid-engined sports car, for export only initially. What was astonishing was that the engine and transmission were Renault products; there were several reasons for this choice, both technical and political.

Obviously, for a car intended to be exported into Europe, it was advantageous to employ a French engine to avoid import duties. There was another reason, too, for Colin Chapman did not wish to put all his eggs in one basket. He had no desire to become totally dependent on Ford for his power units, and he probably felt that a show of independence would be no bad thing at this stage.

Technically, the Renault 16 engine and gearbox had many attractive features for a mid-engined sports car. The standard design was schemed for front-wheel drive, with the engine behind the differential and the gearbox ahead of it. By turning the whole caboodle through 360 degrees, the relative positions of engine, gearbox and final-drive would be identical to those of a Grand Prix car. The only tiny disadvantage would be that there must be four reverse gears and one very slow forward speed!

This could be overcome by mounting the crownwheel on the other side of the pinion, which was later most cleverly achieved without a major redesign. The greatest advantage of this assembly was that the Renault 16 already had its ancillaries and belt drives at the flywheel end of the engine. That meant that they would be in full view on raising the bonnet, instead of hidden up against the bulkhead as in so many mid-engined sports and racing cars.

Furthermore, the engine and gearbox were both of die-cast aluminium, thus saving weight, and the well-known Renault feature of easily changed cast-iron cylinder liners was found, as would be expected. In every way this seemed to be an ideal power-plant for a moderately-priced, road-going sports car, but would the Régie Renault be willing to play?

Luckily, Colin had placed the negotiations in the capable hands of Jabby Crombac, Lotus enthusiast extraordinary and, as the French say, 'plus anglais que les anglais'. Jabby had a staunch ally among the top brass of the Régie in Robert Sicot, who was then in charge of their public relations. Naturally, as we are speaking of France, the negotiations took place in a restaurant, where no doubt the usual drawings were made on the tablecloth, to the despair of the waiters. At these meetings, which were supposed to be secret, Colin was accompanied by Steve Sainville, a research engineer who is now with Novamotor. There was a considerable scare because, purely by chance, a particularly nosey French journalist happened to stroll into the restaurant, but he failed to guess what was going on and so missed a scoop.

It was agreed that, for a start, a mildly tuned version of the Renault 16 engine should be supplied, complete with a gearbox in which the crownwheel and pinion were, of course, transposed. Thus the Lotus Europa became a practicality.

Before discussing this power-unit, it is necessary to remark that it was originally planned that more advanced machinery might be made available in due course, perhaps coupled with

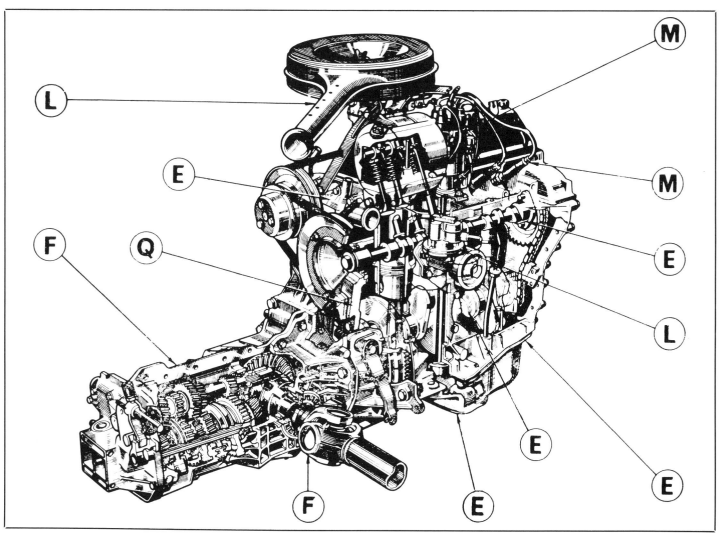

Another cutaway drawing from a Lotus workshop manual, this time displaying the Renault engine and transmission used to drive the Europa mid-engined two-seater. The light-alloy engine has a high camshaft operating the valves through short pushrods and rockers. The ancillaries are mounted at the rear of the engine and accessibility is excellent. The gearbox is of the two-shaft, all-indirect type, the pinion attacking the crownwheel from the rear. A later version of the Renault box, with five speeds, was strong enough to cope with a Lotus twin-cam engine in Sprint tune.

the sacred name of Amédée Gordini. Unfortunately, Jean Redélé of Alpine got wind of these proposals and was not at all pleased. Bob Sicot was able to hold him off and Colin Chapman even made a courtesy visit to the Alpine factory, so all was well, or so it seemed.

The Europa was produced and gave a reasonable performance with the mildly tuned 16 engine. At this point, Bob Sicot received an offer to take up an executive position with Ford France, which he could not refuse. Without his influence, the possibility of obtaining more exciting engines in the future faded, and so although the Renault transmission, in the four-speed and later five-speed form, was retained, the Europa was re-engined with the twin-cam unit from the Elan.

This was a pity, for the ancillaries of the twin-cam had been arranged for a front-engined car and accessibility naturally suffered. The Renault had a high-mounted, chain-driven camshaft, operating the valves through short pushrods and rockers; on the end of this, a large pulley was fitted to drive the ancillaries, as naturally the end of the crankshaft, which carried the flywheel, was not accessible for this purpose.

The big camshaft pulley drove a Vee-belt that passed across the rear of the engine to a small pulley on the water impeller, with a larger pulley alongside it. This drove a small pulley on the alternator, and by this two-stage step-up ratio the latter component was spun at the high revolutions it demanded from the half-speed camshaft. There was no disadvantage in having the belt drives at the bellhousing end of the engine as a fan drive was not required, the radiator being remotely mounted at the front of the car and having its own electric fan. The Renault-engined Europa was the first Lotus to have an alternator instead of a DC generator.

The combined cylinder-block and crankcase was of pressure-die-cast aluminium and carried a sturdy five-bearing counterbalanced crankshaft, to which the flywheel was attached by seven bolts. The camshaft drive was by a duplex roller chain, with a pad-type tensioner on the slack side and anti-flail lugs on the tight side. The valves were operated by pushrods and rockers and were inclined in one plane, to give squish-type combustion chambers.

The cast-iron liners were held down by the light-alloy head and the solid-skirt pistons carried three rings, the lowest one being for oil control. The oil pump, of eccentric rotor type, with a four-lobe inner member turning a five-lobe outer one, was driven by a vertical shaft that obtained its motion from a skew gear on the camshaft; on the top of this shaft was the distributor, which was very accessible, in marked contrast to that of the twin-cam engine! The ports were all on the left side of the head.

The standard engine had dimensions of 76 × 81 mm (1470 cc) and developed 82 bhp at 6,000 rpm. There was also a detuned version for countries with strict exhaust-emission regulations, with dimensions of 77 × 84 mm (1565 cc) and a power output of 80 bhp at 6,000 rpm. The compression ratio was 10.25:1 in both cases and a twin-choke downdraught carburettor was employed, that of the standard engine being a Solex 35 DIDSA 2 and of the emission unit a Solex 26–32 DIDSA 5. Some sources quoted 78 bhp instead of 82 bhp, but the latter figure appears in the Lotus technical literature.

The Renault engine carried a diaphragm-spring clutch which was operated by a very long cable — a rather poor arrangement. The gearbox casing, of pressure-die-cast aluminium, contained a gear cluster of the two-shaft type, giving four synchronized speeds, and the hypoid crownwheel and pinion with the differential. The ratios were 1.03, 1.48, 2.25 and 3.61:1, while that of the final-drive was 3.56:1.

After the Renault engine had been phased-out, this four-speed transmission was used with the twin-cam engine, but not the big-valve version at first, as this was considered to have too much torque. However, when Renault brought out the 16 TX with a 1.65-litre engine, they stressed the five-speed gearbox to take the additional torque of this more powerful unit. The bellhousing to couple the twin-cam engine to the Renault gearbox was a special Lotus component and carried the alternator, which was driven by a large pulley on the end of the inlet camshaft; it also accepted the inner ends of the lower suspension links.

Lotus welcomed the new gearbox with open arms and mated it with their 126 bhp twin-cam engine. This was the power-plant

Installing a Renault engine and gearbox in the back of an early Europa. The ancillaries are belt-driven from a large pulley on the back of the camshaft. By taking the first belt around a small pulley on the back of the water impeller, and a second belt from an adjacent large pulley on to a small pulley on the end of the alternator, it has been possible to drive the latter component at the high revolutions required from the half-speed camshaft.

for the Europa Special, which was introduced in 1972. The ratios were 0.87, 1.21, 1.61, 2.33 and 3.61:1, in conjunction with which a 3.78:1 hypoid was employed. The four-speed box was presumably uprated, too, as it was also offered with the big-valve engine latterly.

These Renault transmissions were used in road-going Europas until the end of the breed in 1975. Like the clutch, the gear-lever had an untidy linkage, which went right past the box and attacked it from the rear. The 47, which was in effect the racing Europa, had a Hewland transmission.

It might be asked why the Hewland gearbox was not used on road-going cars; there are three perfectly good answers to that one. A racing box is too expensive and they are made in very small numbers, while the scream of the straight-toothed pinions would be absolutely intolerable in a closed car like the Europa, for ordinary road work.

CHAPTER 7

The Europa

The mid-engined method

The Lotus Europa was built to satisfy the demand for a mid-engined sports car, which had been inspired by Grand Prix cars of that configuration. It was a fixed-head coupé with vertical fins along the top of the tail, which were probably more cosmetic than aerodynamic. Colin Chapman's original idea was that it should be a cheap road-going sports car and an eventual Seven replacement.

Although the Europa was mid-engined, and in no way resembled the front-engined Elan, there was a very great similarity in the design philosophy and methods of construction. Both cars had a rectangular steel backbone, independently suspended at the four corners and carrying a glass-fibre body. However, while the Elan had its power-unit in front, and a propeller shaft running down the central tunnel of the girder, the Europa placed the engine behind the backs of the driver and passenger.

The chassis frame was welded up from sheet-steel pressings, but was somewhat simpler than that of the Elan because the engine, gearbox and final-drive were all mounted as one unit. The rear of the backbone was split and boxed, spreading into a fork like the front of the Elan, with provision for mounting the engine and gearbox unit between the two prongs.

At the front of the Europa chassis there was no need to increase the width of the backbone, which was directly attached to a box-section cross-member of considerable depth, with ends arranged to support the suspension pivot points. So, the shape of the Europa's central stressed member turned abruptly into a T at the front and more gradually into a Y at the rear waistline. The two rear arms were united at their ends by a tube, which carried the back of the gearbox. There were actually three patterns of tubes and mounting plates, to accommodate the different versions of the Renault transmission, so all Europa frames are not interchangeable.

Though the front suspension was broadly similar to that of the Elan, it differed in many details. In particular, the lower wishbones were cranked instead of being straight and the spring-damper units did not have separate upper mounting points, but pivoted on the centres of the long bolts which formed the inner fulcrums of the upper wishbones. These bolts also carried the links for the bearings of the anti-roll bar. The uprights for the stub-axles had ball-joints at the top and trunnions beneath, as on the Elan.

The steering was by rack-and-pinion with a Triumph Herald telescopic column. Unlike the Elan, the steering gear was not rubber-mounted.

At the rear, the suspension was totally different from that of the Elan. Following the Chapman philosophy of making one part do several jobs, the drive-shafts formed the upper links, these being of the fixed-length type with Hooke's joints. The lower links were straight tubes, pivoting on the rear hub housings and the bellhousing. Fore-and-aft location was by enormously strong box-section steel radius-arms, rigidly bolted to the hub-bearing housings and pivoting on large, chassis-mounted, resilient mountings. It will be appreciated that as the arms of the Y swept in to the central backbone, the radius-arms were similarly angled.

A light steel cross-beam, bolted to the chassis members and

passing over the gearbox, had ears on its ends to take the top bolts of the spring-damper units, which shared the same bolts as the tubular suspension links at their lower ends. As all the lateral forces from the road wheels were transmitted to the gearbox, the resilient mountings of the engine-gearbox unit could not be as soft as those of the Elan.

Another difference between the two cars was in the mounting of the rear brakes. These were located conventionally, close to the wheels, and not on the inner sides of the bearing housings.

The brakes were discs in front and drums behind, the latter being increased in width from $1\frac{1}{4}$ in to $1\frac{1}{2}$ in for the Europa Special. A servo was offered as an extra on the Renault-engined cars, but was standard with the twin-cam power-unit. A single master-cylinder, with no division of the circuits, was employed on the UK market, but twin servos, with separate front and rear systems, were installed for certain countries.

Bolt-on steel road wheels, fitted with 155-13 tyres, were standard, but after the twin-cam engine was adopted larger

The Europa, the first Lotus mid-engined road car, in its initial form, for export only. Subsequently referred to as the Europa S1, these cars are readily identifiable by their one-piece fixed door windows.

A high-angle view of the early Europa showing clearly the characteristic lines of the high-sided body and the pronounced curve of the door windows.

sections became available. Although the steel wheels were still theoretically standard, by the time the Europa Special was on the market it was usual to specify light-alloy wheels, fitted with 175/70-13 front tyres and 185/70-13 at the rear.

The moulded glass-fibre body was constructed in exactly the same way as that of the Elan and full details are given in the chapter on that car. In the case of first-series Europas, called S1, there was one very important difference which proved to be a retrograde step. The body and the chassis were permanently bonded together and could not be separated.

This was all very well from a theoretical point of view, as it resulted in the most rigid structure possible. However, in the event of chassis repairs becoming necessary the difficulties were almost insuperable. In addition, the windows were fixed and the reclining-type seats were non-adjustable.

The idea was that a fairly elaborate ventilation system, in which the front luggage compartment was pressurized as a plenum chamber, would render openable windows redundant.

Nevertheless, how could one ask the way, rebuke another motorist, or explain to a policeman that one hadn't done it?

After nearly three years, these advanced conceptions were abandoned. Most of the S1 Europas had been exported, but when the S2 appeared, in July 1969, it was freely available on the home market. Not only was the body detachable, like that of the Elan, but the windows went up and down electrically and the Grand Prix hammock seats were adjustable. Although the headlamps could not be retracted like those of the Elan, the drag coefficient was phenomenally low at 0.29.

At the front of the body the radiator was offset to the right and angled to exhaust into the wheel-arch. Ahead of it was an electric fan, controlled by a thermal switch, and the small header tank, with a pressurized cap, was in the engine compartment. Circulation was by thermo-syphon, assisted by a belt-driven impeller, and there was the usual engine-mounted thermostat.

In the Renault-engined cars, a single fuel tank was located in the left forward corner of the engine compartment, balancing

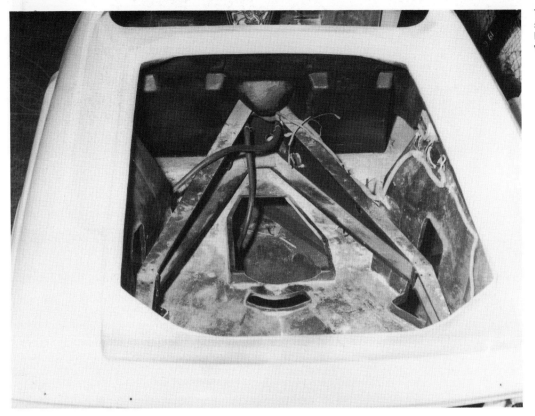

The engine compartment of the Europa showing how the Y-shaped steel backbone straddles the bay and unites with the glass-fibre body shell.

the battery on the other side. This only held about seven gallons, which was generally considered to be rather inadequate. For the twin-cam Europas, the improvements included two tanks situated further back with a total capacity of $12\frac{1}{2}$ gallons, for which there were two filler caps, in addition to an interconnecting pipe. Engine-driven fuel pumps were used with both makes of power-unit and Federal emission equipment was available, with a catch tank and charcoal canister.

The exhaust system for the Renault engine was of the greatest simplicity, with a single downpipe from the manifold, curving back into the silencer and tailpipe. For the twin-cam engine,

there were both cast-iron and fabricated manifolds, with twin downpipes in either case, but the pipes were angled across to the other side of the car before turning into the fore-and-aft-mounted silencer. This was to obtain the theoretical pipe lengths for extraction.

Two twin-choke Weber or Dellorto carburettors were fitted to the twin-cam engine, with two Zenith Strombergs, plus crossover pipes to the exhaust manifold and auxiliary throttles, for Federal emission engines. (This equipment is described in the chapter on the twin-cam engine.) A twin-choke Solex downdraught carburettor was standard equipment for the Renault engine, but again a different type was used in Federal engines.

Although the S1 was a rather basic vehicle, the S2 was quite luxuriously equipped. As well as the speedometer and rev-counter, there were an ammeter, oil-pressure, water tempera-ture and fuel gauges, and the windows were electrically oper-ated. The 12-volt negative-earth electrical system included an alternator, mounted on the Renault engine itself or on the bellhousing of the twin-cam. A single windscreen wiper, with a remote two-speed motor operating the blade through a rack, was always a feature of the Europa. At about the time of the engine change, the fixed headlamps were uprated from 50/40W to 75/70W and the two side fins on the tail were cut down to improve the poor rearward vision, while an air dam beneath the nose added to the stability.

In 1969 the S2 cost £1,667, or £1,275 in kit form, while in 1971 it had gone up to £1,918, or £1,459, including seat belts, but with a brake servo at £20 extra. In 1972 the price with the twin-cam engine was £1,995, or £1,595 as a kit, to which an extra £101 would be added for Brand Lotus light-alloy wheels and Firestone tyres. As the new power unit gave 8% more capacity, 37% more power and 46% more torque, for a weight increase of less than 1 cwt, the smallness of the rise in price was rather remarkable.

However, there was a considerable jump in price when the big-valve engine and other improvements were incorporated, and in 1973 the Europa Special cost £2,471, or £2,044 as a kit. Furthermore, if all the various extras were specified, there was not a great deal of change out of £3,000, tax paid. Compared with the Elan Sprint with the same engine, in fixed-head form, the Europa Special cost some £338 more, as kit cars in both cases, which was a far cry from the original idea of a cheap car to replace the Seven. Their weights were almost identical, with the Elan perhaps a few pounds the heavier, but the Europa was considerably the larger car, being 8 in longer in the wheelbase and 5 in wider in the track, in round figures.

The dimensions of the Europa were: wheelbase 7 ft 8 in, front track 4 ft 5.5 in, rear track 4 ft 5 in, overall length 13 ft 1.5 in, width 5 ft 4.5 in and weight 13.1 cwt (S2) or 14.0 cwt (Special).

For performance figures, let us analyse the road-test reports.

About 109 mph for a lap of the MIRA banked track, and a flying quarter-mile at 115 mph, seem typical maxima, but the 0–60 mph acceleration times vary from 9.5 to 10.7 seconds. These are for the S2 with the Renault engine, but the twin-cam power-unit gave better results, as would be expected.

With the twin-cam engine the Europa was timed one way at 120 mph by both *Motor* and *Autocar*, with laps of MIRA at 116.5

This overhead view of the Europa shows the fixed seating of the first series cars and how the radiator and its electrically operated cooling fan were located remotely from the engine in the nose of the car.

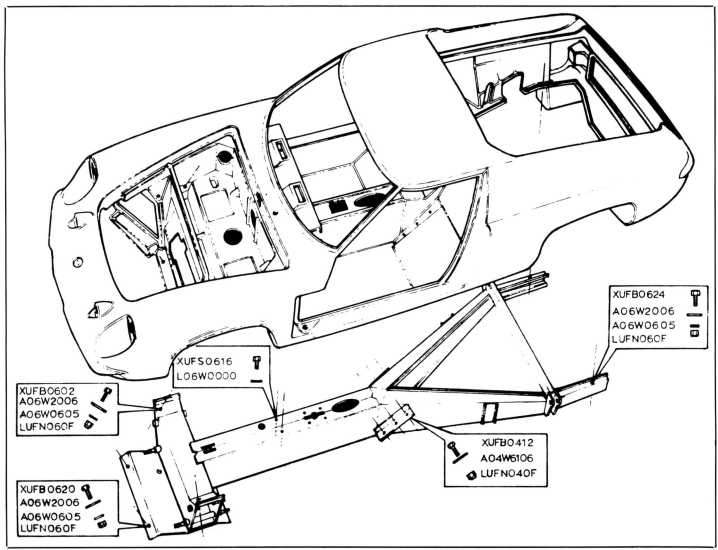

XUFB0624
A06W2006
A06W0605
LUFN060F

XUFS0616
L06W0000

XUFB0602
A06W2006
A06W0605
LUFN060F

XUFB0412
A04W6106
LUFN040F

XUFB0620
A06W2006
A06W0605
LUFN060F

A shortcoming of the first Europas was the bonding together of chassis and body in the interests of greater rigidity, which proved to be not such a good idea when accident damage had to be repaired. For the S2, the body became removable in much the same manner as with the Elan and Plus 2.

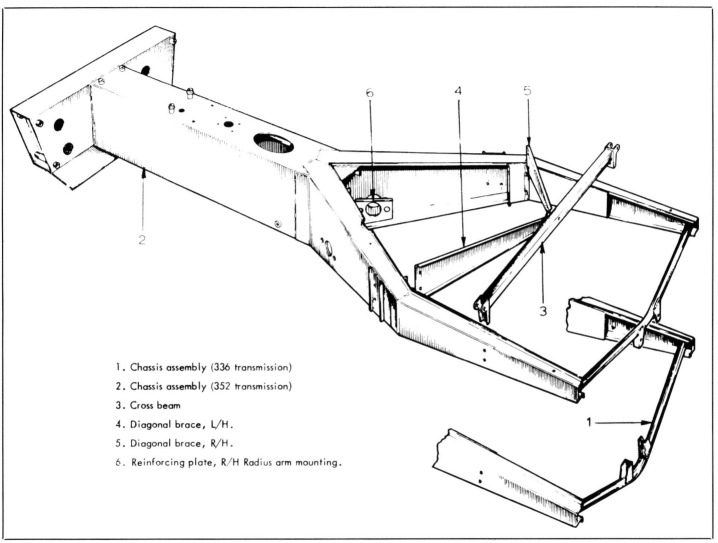

1. Chassis assembly (336 transmission)

2. Chassis assembly (352 transmission)

3. Cross beam

4. Diagonal brace, L/H.

5. Diagonal brace, R/H.

6. Reinforcing plate, R/H Radius arm mounting.

The steel backbone chassis of the Europa. In this case the frame is forked only at the rear as the engine and transmission are in unit. At the front the backbone is welded directly to the cross-member, which is quite massive. The light, separate cross-member, shown detached, bridges the gearbox and provides the upper pivot points for the rear spring-damper units. The alternative end beams are for the different Europa transmissions.

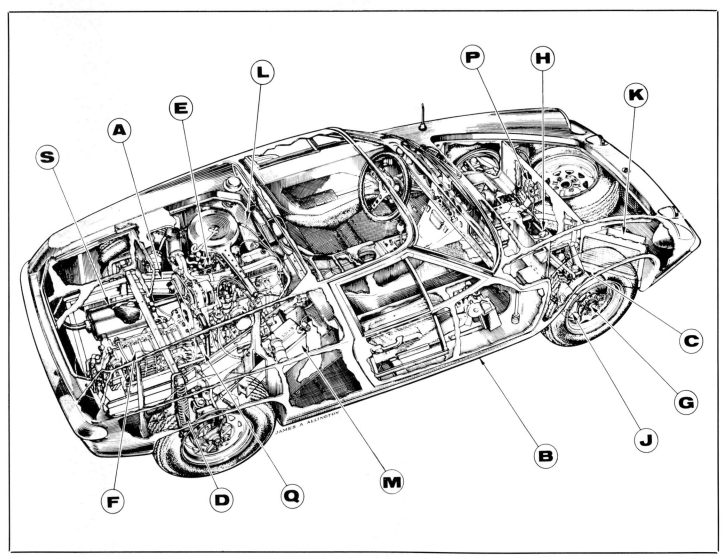

James Allington's excellent cutaway of a Renault-engined Europa S2. The fuel tank is located behind the driver on this left-hand-drive car, with the battery balancing it on the passenger's side. The radiator exhausts into the right front wheel arch.

and 117 mph, but the 0–60 mph acceleration times varied more widely at 8.2 and 7.0 seconds respectively. The Europa Special with the big-valve engine achieved a best quarter-mile for *Motor* of 123.3 mph with a lap of the banked circuit at 121.7 mph, and a 0–60 mph acceleration time of 6.6 seconds. *Autocar* recorded 122 and 121 mph, and again the acceleration varied, their 0–60 mph figure being 7.7 seconds.

Analysing the opinions of road-test drivers over the years, it is at once obvious that the Europa was never such a favourite as the Elan. They were invariably impressed with the roadholding, cornering power and handling qualities of the car, especially when fitted with broader-section tyres behind than in front. The earlier, Renault-engined models were praised for their relatively high maximum speed in spite of a low power output and their remarkable fuel economy was always emphasized.

However, everybody was unanimous in hating the tunnel vision to the rear, caused by the two vertical fins, but even when these were cut down the all-round view was considered poor, and by no means adequate for London traffic on a wet night. Early cars were criticized for bad pedal placing and insufficient foot room, but this was later remedied to some extent.

The very heavy clutch operation, caused by the long cable, was always a point of criticism; one wonders why the hydraulic operation of the 47 was not applied to the road cars. Similarly, the heavy and imprecise gear-change was usually mentioned, though this was improved on later models.

The Press greatly preferred the twin-cam versions and the Renault-engined Europa was likened to a sheep in wolf's clothing. The incredible smoothness of the twin-cam engine was applauded, but the ride was generally regarded as being somewhat less comfortable than that of the Elan, the suspension movement being rather restricted. The earlier reports complained of the noisy exhaust, but this was remedied when the twin-cam engine was adopted. The unwiped corners of the screen, resulting from the use of a single-blade wiper, sometimes earned a mild grumble.

Altogether, the Press had a love-hate relationship with the Europa. This was because Lotus, in choosing the mid-engined configuration, had strayed too closely towards the racing cars

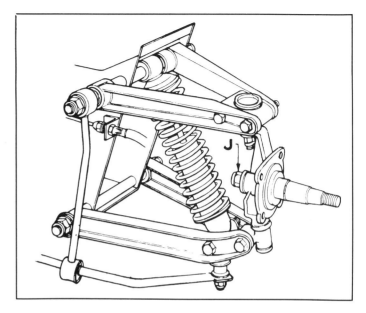

The front suspension of the Europa differs in detail from that of the Elan. The lower wishbones are cranked instead of straight, and the upper pivots of the spring-damper units share the bolts that secure the inboard ends of the upper wishbones and the mountings of the anti-roll bar.

that inspired it. The Europa was therefore not an ideal road car and was very much more effective when developed into the Lotus 47 for competition purposes. On the other hand, the Elan was a comfortable and practical road-going sports car and quite a few motoring writers bought them for their own use, as a result of their road tests.

Naturally, I drove the various Europa models when they were current, but as I have remarked before, memory is not always reliable. So, once again I approached my friends Bell and Colvill, who produced an immaculate five-speed Europa Special, the property of Mrs. Jean Mathieson, who very kindly allowed me to drive it.

The car looked remarkably low and racy, though not beautiful in my opinion. Beauty is in the eye of the beholder, but few

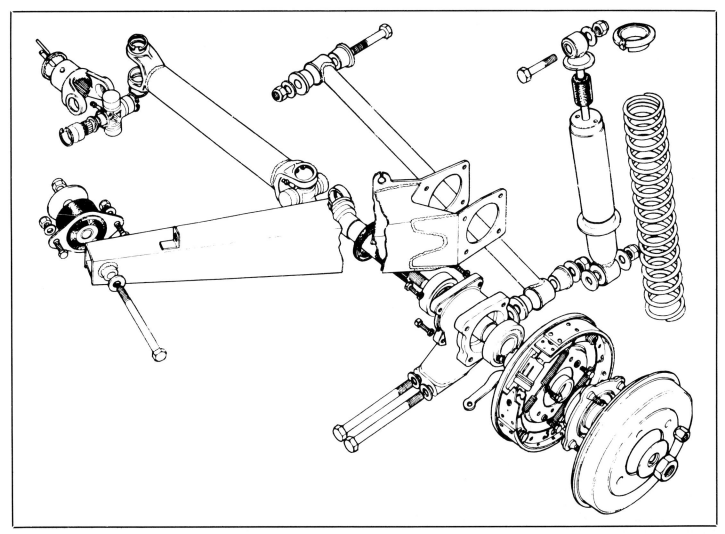

The fixed-length drive-shafts double as the upper links of the rear suspension, with lower light tubular members. Fore-and-aft location is by very sturdy box-section radius arms, which also take the brake torque, and the spring-damper units are mounted between the lower ends of the bearing housings and the detachable bridge-piece across the chassis fork. This rear suspension bears no relationship to that of the Europa-based Lotus 47, which follows single-seater practice.

The somewhat spartan door and interior trim of the S1 Europa. With fixed windows the occupants had to make do with a pressurized ventilation system linked to the front luggage compartment, which acted as a plenum chamber.

A neat exhaust arrangement was adopted for the Renault-engined Europas with the tailpipe emerging inboard of the left rear-light cluster.

Although this Europa retains the high-sided body of the earliest cars, the divided door windows identify it as one of the S2 models with separate body and chassis and many other improvements.

A windcheating shape. Although the headlamps could not be retracted the Europa's drag coefficient was quoted as a remarkable 0.29 when the car was announced.

mid-engined cars convey that poetry of motion, that suggestion of a greyhound straining at the leash, which Ettore Bugatti, for one, was able to capture.

One had to crouch right down to enter, but once inside there was a reasonable amount of room. The all-round view was acceptable and the rather blind rear quarters did not worry me on the roads of Surrey, though it might have been a different story in London traffic. However, I must endorse all the criticisms of the clutch operation, for it was both very heavy and sticky, tending to move in a series of jerks, while the awkward angle of the pedal compounded the felony. It seems extraordinary that this ha'porth of tar was allowed to spoil the ship for so long. The gear-change was not of the knife-through-butter vari-

ety, if I may use another *cliché*, but although it tended to feel rather unfriendly on first acquaintance, I think one would soon become accustomed to it.

Predictably, the traction was excellent and racing starts were easy. The engine was smooth, flexible and had any amount of torque, while the acceleration was impressive. Yet, it was not quite so brilliant as that of an Elan Sprint, which was probably a matter of gear ratios. Where the Europa beat the Elan was in high-speed cruising, and that fifth gear made all the difference.

Mid-engined cars have often been criticized for their high interior noise level, but the Europa, though not a particularly quiet machine, was not unreasonably noisy by sports-car stan-

In S2 form the Europa still relied on the Renault engine and transmission. As can be seen in this picture the high body sides behind the cockpit constituted a considerable interference with rearward vision.

During the course of the S2's production life the front lighting arrangements were modified with the indicator lights being semi-recessed in neat nacelles inboard of the headlamps.

The substantial improvement to the cockpit of the Europa S2 included a much-modified dashboard layout with wood facing for the instrument panel and fully trimmed doors with recessed release handles, changes which were carried forward on to the later Twin Cam model.

dards. It was superior to some other cars of this configuration, inasmuch as it did not tend to lock its front wheels during heavy braking, though I did not have an opportunity to try it on wet roads.

The steering was light and direct, giving plenty of feel of the road surface. In my short test drive I did not succeed in breaking away the rear-end, but I'm quite sure that the quick steering would make correction easy. The car was very well balanced and fast through corners, though not appreciably faster than an Elan, as has sometimes been alleged. Its only vice was a tendency to wander a little on the straight, when driven fast on inferior roads.

With one luggage boot in front, plus a box above the transmission, the Europa was by no means so impractical as some sports cars of this ilk. Nevertheless, for me it lacked the charac-

ter of the Elan and I am in no doubt which car I would prefer to have. Still, there are those for whom the mid-engine position is a must, and for them it's the Europa every time.

To re-cap, the Europa story went something like this. The S1 (Lotus 46), which was theoretically for export only, was built in 1966 and 1967, with the Renault 16 engine and transmission. The S2 (Lotus 54), was an improved version with a detachable chassis, of which production started in 1967. In 1969 it was on sale in the UK and in 1970 a Federal-bodied Europa was exported to the USA (Lotus 65). In 1971 came the twin-cam Europa, with Lotus engine and four-speed Renault gearbox (Lotus 74). It was succeeded by the Europa Special at the end of 1972, which had the big-valve twin-cam engine, usually with the five-speed Renault gearbox. The type was phased-out in 1975, after a total production of 9,230 cars.

Cut-down sides and Brand Lotus 'spider' wheels were the most easily distinguishable features of the Europa Twin Cam on its announcement in 1971. The Ford-based engine meant an increase in power output from 82 to 105 bhp, and a bib spoiler was added at the front to improve high-speed stability.

The Twin Cam was equipped with twin fuel tanks, each with its separate filler, giving a combined capacity of 12½ Imperial gallons compared with the 7-gallon capacity of the Renault-engined cars. The exhaust pipe no longer emerges through the bodywork.

The Europa Special, introduced in 1972 with the 126 bhp Big Valve version of the twin-cam engine, marked the zenith of Europa production. As well as the mechanical changes the opportunity was taken to tidy up the body sides below the doors. This example is finished in black and gold in honour of John Player, who were to remain the major sponsors of the Lotus Grand Prix team until the end of 1978.

The announcement of the Europa Special brought a further refinement in the car's interior, notably in the use of softer trim materials. The two switches flanking the central ashtray are the controls for the electric window lifts.

A clearer view of the instrument and control layout of the Europa Special. The two controls recessed into the padded central armrest are the choke and the temperature control knob for the heater. This is the meticulously maintained car, owned by Mrs. Jean Mathieson, which is another of the trio of cars photographed on the jacket of this book.

The engine compartment of the same car. The camshaft drive is hard up against the forward bulkhead and inevitably accessibility is not as good as with the earlier Renault engine. However, routine servicing of carburettors, battery and the engine's oil needs presents no difficulties, while a plug change is straightforward once the cover plate has been unbolted.

CHAPTER 8

The Lotus 47

Europa-based sports prototype

The Lotus 47 made its dramatic appearance at the Boxing Day Brands Hatch meeting in 1966, when John Miles drove it to victory in the unlimited sports car race, which it won outright against more powerful machinery. At that time, it was sometimes called a Europa, after the production model from which it was derived, but the difference was so great that it was later known simply by its type number. Let us not forget that the 47 was contemporary with the Renault-engined S1 Europa, the twin-cam road-going Europa being five years in the future.

The 47 was a sports prototype, intended for racing in the FIA Group 4 category. To be eligible for this class, 50 cars had to be produced, or at least laid down for production. Accordingly Lotus Components Ltd., a subsidiary of Lotus, made or acquired the necessary parts for a considerable number of cars. They built the team cars for factory participation in races, and many kits were assembled by outside constructors.

No doubt the FIA were satisfied that enough components had been made for the 47 to be officially homologated, and I would not like to suggest that they were deceived. Nevertheless, it seems unlikely that the full 50 were ever completed and only about 25 or 30 were actively campaigned, though others were probably adapted for road use.

The chassis-frame broadly resembled that of the Europa, though it was of slightly lighter construction — too light as it turned out. The glass-fibre, fixed-head coupé body was also a lightened version of the S1 Europa shell. As in the Europa, the central chassis backbone spread out into two arms, forming a Y, between which the centrally-mounted engine and gearbox nestled.

Replacement of the Renault engine and transmission by a racing twin-cam unit and a Hewland gearbox, naturally called for some changes. The arms of the Y were shortened and a box-section cross-member was welded to the two ends. It spread out in the centre, forming a hoop to provide an aperture through which the forward end of the transmission housing passed, a pair of hefty lugs above the differential accepting two large bolts from the top part of the said cross-member. The front engine mounts were on the two arms of the Y.

Like the Europa, the rear Y was joined by the box-section backbone to a front T. The forward cross-member was very deep and carried the front suspension, rack-and-pinion steering and pedal box. Proprietary suspension components, as used on the Triumph Vitesse, were employed in front. The lower wishbones were assembled from two steel pressings on to the fixed axis bars, on which they pivoted, that were welded into the front box at a castor angle of $3°$ to the horizontal. At their outer ends, the lower wishbones carried the trunnions of the uprights for the stub-axles, also the lower pivots for the spring-damper units.

The upper wishbones were forgings and their axis bars were in the form of large bolts, which were located by welded-in bushes in the cross-member and carried the upper bearings of the spring-damper units, also the links in which the anti-roll bar pivoted. These wishbones located the uprights in ball-joints, which were adjustable for camber angle.

Rubber bushes for the suspension were standard, usually replaced by metal-to-metal, with Rose joints where appropriate.

One of the first Lotus 47s emerging from Druid's hairpin at Brands Hatch during a track test for the former monthly magazine *Motor Racing,* with John Blunsden in the cockpit normally occupied by Jack Oliver or John Miles.

The rack-and-pinion gear was coupled by short, ball-jointed track rods to steering arms bolted to the stub-axles. The platform height of the front springs and the damper settings were adjustable.

At the rear, the suspension geometry was entirely different from that of the road-going Europa. The light-alloy uprights came from the Lotus 59 single-seater and the disc brakes were located on their inner sides, remote from the wheels. The drive-shafts no longer doubled as suspension links, having rubber-doughnut joints at their inboard ends, and there were single, tubular top links, with reversed wishbones beneath. There were two longer tubular trailing-arms either side, pivoting near the front of the engine. The rear suspension was fully adjustable (except the trailing-arms) and Rose-jointed throughout. Suspension loads were fed into the hoop-shaped rear cross-member, which also carried the anti-roll bar.

There were disc brakes all round, with dual circuits, twin master-cylinders and a balance bar. The clutch operation was also hydraulic, an enormous improvement over the long cable of the Europa. The body was that of the Europa S1, with fixed seats, but the plastic windows could be propped open at the rear for ventilation.

The engine fitted by the works, with which the car was homologated, was the Mark 13C Lotus Cosworth. The team cars had Tecalemit-Jackson fuel-injection, but private owners seemed unable to cope with this. Most of them eventually reverted to Weber 45 carburettors, but in one or two cases the very expensive Lucas injection system was fitted.

The twin-cam engine had dimensions of 83.5 × 72.75 mm (1594 cc) and developed about 165 bhp at 7,000 rpm on a compression ratio of 11:1. Special racing pistons were used, with Dykes top rings, plain second compression rings and split oil-control rings with expanders. Dry-sump lubrication was installed. The aluminium cylinder-head gave an included valve angle of 54° and the inlets were of 1.53 in diameter, with 1.32 in for the exhausts. Cosworth double valve springs were used and the valve timing was as follows:

Inlet opens	46° B.T.D.C.
Inlet closes	78° A.B.D.C.
Exhaust opens	70° B.B.D.C.
Exhaust closes	54° A.T.D.C.

Those were the basic Cosworth figures, but they may well have varied in engines prepared by other tuners, such as BRM and Vegantune. Other makes of power-unit were also used in the 47, including Coventry Climax.

The clutch was a special diaphragm-spring $7\frac{1}{2}$ in Borg and Beck. The gearbox, which incorporated the crownwheel, pinion and differential, was a Hewland FT 200 five-speed unit. The Lotus remote (very!) gear-change had a central lever on the tunnel, with first left and back, opposite reverse, and the other four in the usual order. An alternator was belt-driven from the gearbox and various different positions were tried for this component.

Like the Europa, the radiator was ahead of the right front wheel-arch, into which it exhausted. In the 47, an oil cooler was mounted with it, and the dry-sump oil tank was ahead of the passenger's feet. There were two catch tanks, one for the oil tank and one for the engine breather.

The fuel was carried in two light-alloy tanks behind the bulkhead, with quick-release filler caps projecting from each side of the car, the total capacity being 20 gallons. These fed into a valved collector tank, in the undertray just behind the driver, which avoided starvation due to cornering and braking forces. In the case of the works cars, an electric pump fed the fuel-injection system.

The centre-locking, magnesium-alloy wheels had peg drive and three-eared spinners. Various sizes were used, starting with $7\frac{1}{2} \times 13$ in front and 10×13 in rear, followed by $8\frac{1}{2} \times 13$ in front and 12×13 in rear. Tyres normally used were Dunlop $475 \times 100 \times 13$ front and $600 \times 1200 \times 13$ rear. For wet conditions, Goodyear road tyres were often used on 6×13 in front and $8\frac{1}{2} \times 13$ in rear wheels.

The centre part of the body behind the cockpit removed to reveal generous working space above and around the Lotus twin-cam engine and the Hewland FT200 transaxle through which it delivered its 165 brake horsepower.

Two views of Nick Atkins' immaculate Lotus 47, which began its career as a Group 4 sports prototype and now enjoys a new lease of competitive life with, hopefully, many more years ahead of it in events catering for the better competition cars of yesteryear.

The spartan but functional interior of the early Lotus 47. Points of criticism during the track test were the closeness of the pedals and the lack of any foot rest to the left of the clutch.

This view of the cockpit of Nick Atkins' car makes an interesting comparison with the earlier car. The entire dashboard and console area has been finished in non-reflective matt paint, a smaller-diameter and more comfortable steering wheel has been fitted, the gear lever is shorter, the clutch and brake pedals are more widely spaced and a left foot rest has been added.

As originally built, the cars proved suitable only for short races. However, the factory developed a couple of cars for long-distance racing and one of them won the 2-litre class in the BOAC 500 in the hands of John Miles and Jackie Oliver, the Porsches having expired. These cars formed the basis of an improved model called 47A, which had much better brakes and a greatly strengthened chassis. The detachable body shell of the Europa S2 was adopted, and the seats were no longer fixed.

Many private owners modified their earlier cars to improve reliability and stamina. I have discussed these modifications with some drivers, and particularly with Nick Atkins, who has helped me tremendously with this chapter. Nick has been a fervent admirer and an impassioned driver of the 47 for many years, and he keeps a register of all the current owners. He has also passed on to me some most helpful notes from Victor Walker, who has campaigned a 47 with great effect.

It would appear that a well-prepared engine will stand an enormous amount of thrashing, and that goes for the gearbox, too. The weak points are the brakes, which used to suffer terminal fading incredibly soon and limited the cars to ten-lap races as an absolute maximum. The chassis had various weak points, which were prone to cracking, and the suspension needed attention, while the rubber doughnuts were too close to the gearbox and tended to rub against it.

The original equipment was $9\frac{1}{8}$ in discs and iron calipers, which were hopeless. These should be replaced with $10\frac{1}{2}$ in discs and AR Mk 2 calipers, with adapter brackets, using Ferodo DS11 pads. The ultimate was to mount three-pot calipers with suitable sandwich plates. Several 47 owners have thrown away their doughnuts and replaced the drive-shafts, either with

Rear view showing the final-drive and rear suspension arrangements of the Nick Atkins car. Note that the fixed drive-shafts with Rotoflex doughnut couplings at their inner end, which were part of the original specification of the Lotus 47, have been replaced by sliding-spline shafts with Hooke's joints at each end.

Hooke's joints and sliding splines or with those constant-velocity joints that can absorb plunging movements. This conversion makes it possible to use inboard rear brakes.

There was a tendency for cracks to appear in the front cross-member of the chassis, around the welded-in bushes for the large bolts forming the top wishbone axis bars and the spring-damper anchorages. Victor Walker overcame this by boxing-in from the lower wishbone locating joint, leaving just enough clearance for the spring to operate. Chassis flexing had also caused cracks in the area where the hooped cross-member was welded to the chassis arms, and he formed a box-section at each end by welding in gussets. He also braced the lower radius-arm front pickup points to the lower part of the rear chassis hoop with $\frac{1}{4}$ in steel tubes, and the anchorage point of the inverted bottom wishbone was strengthened and bracketed to the hoop, which was reinforced as a jacking point.

Walker replaced the engine mountings, both on the engine itself and the chassis, with heavier-gauge ones. While he was at

The front body section raised to reveal the trio of pedal master-cylinders, washer reservoir, oil tank and oil cooler, the latter being mounted adjacent to the water radiator in the front wheel-arch area.

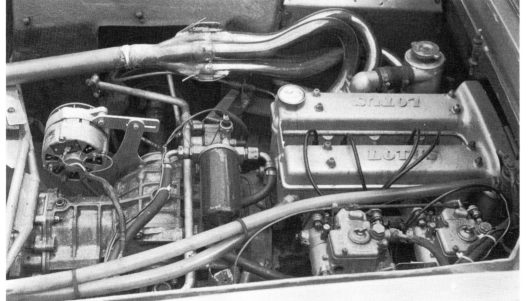

Another view of the rear compartment of the Nick Atkins car showing how the alternator is belt-driven from a pulley on the left output shaft of the transaxle, just outboard of the mounting plate. The rear chassis hoop, which straddles the bellhousing, provides a convenient mounting for the cylindrical oil filter.

Three views of the Lotus 62, a tubular-framed logical development of the Europa and Lotus 47 theme, which was used as a mobile test bed for the experimental Vauxhall-related 2-litre Lotus LV 220 racing engine. Only two cars were built, with a wheelbase of 91 inches and an unladen weight of approximately 1,350 lb.

A rare view of a rare car revealing the pronounced door cut-outs in the roof section of the Lotus 62, together with fixing arrangements for the lift-up front and rear body sections and the various air intake and extractor ducts.

The Lotus 62 had sprouted a large rear spoiler as well as long, slim, high-mounted front fins in place of the original rounded type by the time John Miles had a wet drive at the 1969 Martini meeting at Silverstone. Brian Muir and Roy Pike were also engaged to drive the Gold Leaf-sponsored cars, but the programme was abandoned when shortcomings in the touring car cylinder block were discovered, whereupon Lotus turned their attention to the development of their own 2-litre engine.

it he made some chassis modifications to give better accessibility to the dry-sump pumps, chain tensioner and distributor, as well as facilitating engine removal. It was desirable to stiffen the pedal-box mountings, as a terrified driver can exert an enormous effort on the brake pedal!

Some stiffening of the suspension links was advantageous, such as boxing-in the lower front wishbones and strengthening the lower rear radius-arm. It must be remembered that the front suspension uprights and stub-axles are mass-production parts, which were never intended for the rigours of racing, so frequent examination and occasional replacement is advisable.

The 47 and 47A raced internationally in 1967 and 1968, after which they were no longer competitive in international sports car events against cars with full 2-litre engines. However, they are still actively campaigned by enthusiasts and can put up a formidable performance in sprints and short races. Now, they are becoming 'historic', and those owners who have hung on to them are in possession of appreciating assets. This is excellent, because it will save them from being converted into road cars — a fate worse than death, for which they are totally unsuited and not even legal under the latest regulations.

Although it is really outside the scope of this book, perhaps I may mention the Lotus 62, of which two were made. The body was a coupé rather like the 47, but with a rounded tail and wheelarches for Formula 1 wheels and tyres, and the front and rear body sections hinged to open. It was not, in fact, related to the 47, having a tubular spaceframe instead of a backbone.

The engine consisted of a Vauxhall Victor 2-litre slant-4 cast-iron cylinder-block, with a Lotus 16-valve head. It developed 220 bhp at 8,000 rpm and was mated to a ZF five-speed gearbox. It won its class at the BOAC 500, driven by John Miles and Brian Muir, and Miles was third in the TT. In the Trophy of the Dunes, at Zandvoort, the cars were fourth and sixth. This was in the nature of a research project, at the design stage of the new Lotus light-alloy engine, and no further cars were produced.

Finally, a car much closer to the 47 was a special luxury coupé, built for GKN. This mid-engined car had the backbone lengthened by three inches to accommodate a 3.5-litre Rover V8

engine, tuned to give 185 bhp. The racing gearbox being too noisy for road use, a ZF five-speed transmission was adopted. The machine was intended both for test purposes and as a fun-car for the top brass, and it was baptized Lotus 47D — I am delighted that it is being preserved as a part of the G. A. Vandervell collection.

The modified Rover V8 engine of the Lotus 47D, installed in an enlarged Europa body shell to provide a high-speed test bed for components manufactured by the GKN Group of Companies.

GKN's purpose-built Lotus 47D at Silverstone. After extensive development by Vandervell Products Ltd., a member of the GKN Group, the Rover engine, which was bored and stroked to 4.4 litres, delivered 292 bhp at 7,000 rpm to give the car a remarkable 0 to 100 mph acceleration time of 11.1 seconds and a top speed of around 180 mph.

CHAPTER 9

Elans and 47s in competition

Chequered Flag sets the pace

No attempt will be made to list all the races in which Lotus Elans and 47s have taken part. It would be a stupendous undertaking and, in any case, it would be out-of-date before the ink was dry, as the cars are still being raced by enthusiastic owners. Therefore, a more general treatment is, perhaps, indicated.

Although the 47 was intended as a competition car, the Elan was definitely not. It was Colin Chapman's intention that it should be a quiet and comfortable road-going sports car at a reasonable price, and nothing more. However, owners at once started to enter their new machines in races, and serious deficiencies in the roadholding department were at once apparent. Clearly, something had to be done about it.

The Elan was greatly admired for its handling and roadholding under ordinary road conditions. However, nobody except a maniac drives at ten-tenths on the public highway, and in any case, normal tyres cannot develop the cornering power of racing rubber. Among the teams which endeavoured to race Elans was Graham Warner's Chequered Flag outfit. He undertook an intensive programme of development on the cars, and eventually Lotus themselves marketed a competition version, called Lotus 26R, which was largely developed from Graham Warner's experience.

The racing Elans had special lightweight bodies, with thinner glass-fibre panels. With engines developing well over 140 bhp and tyres that could put that power on to the road, excessive flexibility was found in many parts and even actual breakages occurred. The first recorded appearance of the Elan in a race was when Graham Warner drove a machine, bearing his own personal registration number, LOV 1, in the Silverstone International Trophy meeting on May 11, 1963. *Autosport's* reporter wrote, 'once handling problems have been overcome, it will be a strong contender for 2-litre honours'.

Jackie Stewart, who with Mike Spence shared the driving with Graham, put it more strongly, describing the racing Elan as, 'the most difficult little sod of a car I have ever driven'. The primary alteration was to mount the steering rack solidly and to do away with all the rubber in the suspension pivots. Metal-to-metal bearings were employed, with Rose-joints where appropriate. These changes made the cars unpleasant for normal road use, with a high interior noise level, and stiffer suspension settings spoilt the comfortable ride, but the road holding began to improve.

The increased cornering loads that were fed into the frame called for some stiffening, and this was particularly the case with the tubular lower links of the rear suspension, which were strengthened and made more rigid. For racing, an adjustment was provided to set the toe-out of the wheels. The rubber-doughnut universal-joints resented the extra power of the Cosworth-built twin-cam engine and they were a great source of unreliability. It will be understood that the results of a drive-shaft breaking free and flailing around could be catastrophic, so the drivers heaved sighs of relief when orthodox universal and slip-joints were adopted.

In the Chequered Flag cars, the radiators were moved forward and air was supplied through NACA ducts to the twin-choke Weber carburettors. Weight was saved by replacing the

The Chequered Flag's black-and-white Elan in action at Goodwood in 1964 with Mike Spence chasing Dickie Stoop's Porsche 904 GTS through the chicane — a favourite spectator viewing point on the sadly missed racing circuit. Photograph courtesy *Autosport*.

Elans in the wet at Silverstone with Gabrielle Konig holding off a challenge from Jeff Edmonds. Note the lack of a front bumper on the leading car, also the wider wheels with fatter tyres. A Patrick Benjafield photograph courtesy *Autosport*.

An exciting GT race at Crystal Palace in 1965 with Jackie Oliver and his Elan holding the narrowest of leads over Bertorelli's modified Lotus 15 and Boley Pittard's Alfa Romeo chasing them both through North Tower Crescent. Photograph courtesy *Autosport.*

A SMART Elan of the Stirling Moss Automobile Racing Team, with Valerie Pirie, for many years the maestro's secretary, putting her boss' tuition to good effect as she swings out of the Goodwood chicane. Photograph courtesy *Autosport*.

Another Elan with a different profile above the waistline, this time one of the Team Surbiton Motors cars incorporating an attractive fastback conversion on the start line at Crystal Palace with Barry Wood at the wheel.

A trio of Elans scrambling through the Esses at Croft during the 1966 Whit Monday meeting with T. E. Blackadder leading R. G. Smith and G. Durham. Photograph courtesy *Autosport*.

It seems that at times GT regulations were interpreted fairly leniently in 1965. Here is Ray Parsons working hard in his Elan to hold off Tony Beeson's Lotus 23 through Druids Bend at Brands Hatch. Photograph courtesy *Autosport*.

An Elan sandwich at Zandvoort with Graham Warner in the Chequered Flag 'LOV 1' chasing Andrew Hedges' special MG Midget into the banked Hunzerug bend while a Ferrari is about to attack another Elan from the rear. Photograph courtesy *Autosport*.

pop-up headlamps with small fixed units, but these were really too low to be legal for road use. All the development work began to pay dividends, and Warner was fourth in a race at Goodwood behind three Ferraris, but at the Silverstone GP meeting he rammed Michael Parkes' Ferrari on the starting line. At the same meeting, Rodney Banting's Elan touched Alan Hutcheson's MGB, causing both cars to crash spectacularly, but the drivers were not badly hurt.

Another team early in the field with the Elan was the SMART of Stirling Moss. They had a light green hardtop which Sir John Whitmore drove, and he won the 2½-litre GT event at the BRSCC International Brands Hatch meeting. However, in 1963 most private owners still had roadholding problems with Elans.

In 1964, the privateers were beginning to understand Elan roadholding requirements, and they flooded the circuits at Club events, though reliability was not always achieved. The Chequered Flag team was joined by Ian Walker's beautiful 'Gold Bug' Elans, driven by Peter Arundell and Mike Spence, the latter still having an occasional drive with the Flag team. Jackie Stewart won many Club events and was fourth in the Prix de Paris at Montlhéry.

Mike Beckwith was successful in an Elan entered by Chris Barber, and among the most prominent owner-drivers were Jackie Oliver, John Lepp, Malcolm Wayne, Sid Taylor, Dick Crosfield and Rex Willoughby. *Autosport* described the Elan 26R as the ideal costume for the 1600 division.

In 1965, Home and Wehrle came fifth with their Elan in the South African Nine Hours race, and John Lepp was also fifth,

Ian Walker, whose North London-based company is now responsible for the official reconditioning of Lotus twin-cam engines, posing with a special-bodied car which he prepared for endurance racing and which he had hoped to run at Le Mans. A Michael Cooper photograph courtesy *Autosport.*

The competition debut of the Lotus 47 came at the dull and damp Boxing Day meeting at Brands Hatch in 1966, when John Miles had a runaway victory in the special GT race against light opposition. Photograph courtesy *Autosport*.

Jackie Oliver checks a spot of oversteer on the Lotus Components entered Lotus 47 which he shared with John Miles in the 1967 BOAC 500 at Brands Hatch; they took a convincing victory in the 2-litre prototype class. Note the twin air intakes sprouting from the engine cover. Photograph courtesy *Autosport*.

against much larger cars, in the Goodwood Whit-Monday sports car race. John Hine won the big Dunlop International race at Zandvoort and Jochen Neerpasch was second, both in Elans, while John Harris and Dick Crosfield won the *Autosport* Championship with their Elan.

Elan drivers were becoming extremely successful on the Club scene, and Jeff Edmonds had 13 wins. Other winners were Geoff Breakell, Pat Ferguson, Malcolm Wayne, John Lepp, Digby Martland, Carlos Gaspar and Willie Green. Also among the front-runners were John Calvert, Keith Burnand, Peter Creasey, Mark Konig and his wife Gabrielle, while Gerry Marshall graduated from his Mini to an Elan, with some success.

In 1966, John Miles drove an Elan entered by Willment, and this was perhaps the apogee of the model in racing. The car had a BRM Phase 2 version of the Lotus twin-cam engine, which eventually developed 158 bhp. The summary of Miles' season was that he competed at eight circuits in 14 races and finished in all of them. He won 10 outright, won his class in 12, and was second in class in two, taking six lap records. At the end of the season he then won the *Autosport* Championship. Other winners in Elans that year were Bob Ellice, Keith Burnand, Bill Dryden and Eric Oliver, the famous sidecar man.

At the Boxing Day Brands Hatch meeting, John Miles won the first time out with the Lotus 47, entered by Lotus Components Ltd. The weather was wet, and from what we know of the original brakes perhaps it was just as well!

Lotus rivalry with Bill Dryden and his Elan battling it out with John Blades and his Lotus 47 at Ingliston during a Special GT race in 1967. A W. K. Henderson photograph courtesy *Autosport*.

John Miles in the immaculate works-entered Lotus 47 carrying the new Golf Leaf Team Lotus colours which were adopted in 1968. In the supporting GT race at the International Trophy meeting at Silverstone Miles finished second to Tony Dean's Porsche Carrera 6 in the 2-litre class.

In 1967, John Miles won eight firsts in British events with the 47. After much development, the car was made more suitable for long-distance races and John Miles and Jackie Oliver shared a 47 to finish ninth in the BOAC Six Hours race, winning the 2-litre class; however, four other 47s failed to finish. At Villa Real, Portugal, Carlos Santos and Noguira Pinto were second and third in 47s after a 5.5-litre Lola-Chevrolet, with Don Marriott finishing fourth behind them in an Elan. At a Montlhéry meeting in September, Robert Hubs secured fifth place with a 47, while in the Laurenço Marques Three Hours race, Jack Holme's similar car was fourth behind a Lola-Chevrolet and two Ford GT40s, and sixth in the Roy Hesketh race, in South Africa, with Richie Jute as co-driver.

In concluding the 1967 results, let us not forget the Elans, and it is surely worth recording that at a Group 4 race on the Mallory Park circuit they took the first six places, the lucky men being Peter Jackson, Robert Ellice, John Calvert, George Humble, Keith Burnand and Mike Crabtree.

In 1968, John Player announced that they would be sponsoring 47s in 35 races. John Miles and Jackie Oliver won many awards, but John Hine and Trevor Taylor were often forced to retire. Highlights were John Miles' class win and sixth overall with a 47 at the Players Trophy, Silverstone, and Jackie Oliver's identical result in the Guards Trophy at Brands Hatch. At Montes Claros, Portugal, John Miles was third in the 47, with a class win, and Jackie Oliver was sixth at Croft, again winning the class. At Laurenço Marques Jack Holm this time used an Elan to finish sixth, partnered by John Rowe, while at home Keith Holland was very successful in Club events with his 47.

Thereafter, the 47 met with diminishing success in the face of tougher competition. Now it has become a Historic Sports Car and no doubt has plenty of events ahead of it, while the value of an unmodified example must increase. It's a nice car for enthusiasts to run, because of the help that Nick Atkins gives to owners who are on his register.

The original smooth Elan silhouette has given way to exaggerated appendages in the quest for greater aerodynamic downforce now that the cars qualify for Modsports racing. This is Nicky Ellis's highly decorated and successful car at Croft during a 1979 race. A Paul Boothroyd photograph courtesy *Autosport*.

Paul Berman's wide-wheeled 1.8-litre Modsports Elan nosing ahead of Richard Gamble's Marcos during a race at Oulton Park in 1979. Berman went on to finish second to Jon Fletcher's similar car. A Peter McFadyen photograph courtesy *Autosport*.

Modsports racing has provided a new competition opportunity for the Europa. Here is Duncan Hall's 1.8-litre Europa Special in pursuit of Brian Stevenson's Davrian in a successful battle for second place at Ingliston in October 1979 behind John Fyda's 2-litre Elan. A W. K. Henderson photograph courtesy *Autosport*.

CHAPTER 10

Buying an Elan, Europa or Plus 2

The choice and the maintenance

Let's start with the easy one. If you're thinking of buying an S1 Europa — don't! That was the model in which the body and chassis could not be separated, so quite a small accident might make it a virtual write-off. Worse still, a secondhand (or tenth-hand!) car may already have had its quota of crashes, and highly immoral methods of repair have probably been used. It is more than likely that everything is out of line and that the suspension and steering geometry are not as designed, to put it mildly.

Luckily, most of the S1 Europas went abroad and the later models have detachable chassis, like the Elan and the +2. All these Lotus models are now becoming collectors' pieces, especially the Elan, for nothing quite like it is built nowadays. A really mint Elan may already be worth twice what it cost, and prices are rising.

Because the Elan is exceptionally fast for its small size and light weight, chassis tuning is unusually critical. An Elan that is set up according to the book is a delightfully responsive instrument and the handling is impeccable. Any slight imperfection, however, such as the steering rack being at an incorrect height or the rear wheels out of track, may make it handle worse than any old banger. The other models with their wider track are not quite so critical, but the same dictum applies to a lesser extent. So, if you are paying a high price, you must check the handling and roadholding, for these are the qualities that lift the race-bred Lotus far above other cars.

There are really two things that you can do. You can acquire a mint example and live happily ever after, or you can buy a car that is obviously in need of attention and rebuild it from the floor up. Such an exercise can be highly rewarding, not only because a rebuilding job can be most enjoyable, but because if the work is well done the car will be worth a lot of money. The important thing is not to pay much for an ill-maintained Lotus, for it's only the mint ones that fetch high prices.

The repair of glass-fibre bodies is now well understood and their freedom from rust is an enormous advantage. Should a complete section of the body be required, Lotus keep these and they are all catalogued, with illustrations, in the spare-parts lists. For most normal repairs, however, it's merely a case of laying on glass-fibre in the approved manner. Refinishing is also straightforward as Lotus bodies are not self-coloured, apart from the silver roofs of certain +2 models.

The chassis frame is also easy to recondition and should be checked most carefully for being in line. Simple welding can be used, as no unusual steels were incorporated. It is necessary to emphasize that it is not generally advisable to weld the front cross-member. This is because it forms a vacuum reservoir for the pop-up headlamps, and petrol invariably seeps back from the induction system, in spite of the non-return valve. This petrol becomes absorbed in the pores of the metal and, even though it appears to be dry, a violent explosion may take place as soon as the welding torch goes into action.

When a fair amount of money is being spent on a complete rebuild, one should consider the advisability of having a new chassis-frame. These are not expensive by modern standards, and a frame that has already been knocked about a bit, with obvious signs of inexpert straightening or welding, will need a deal of work before it is anything like true. There are drainage holes at the front corners, and if these have become blocked water may have collected and weakened the steel by rusting.

Lotus state that they are the only people who have the proper jigs to construct chassis-frames, upon which they make a small batch from time to time, as spares for their earlier models. There are apparently some non-genuine frames around that have not been made on the official jigs, and these should be regarded with deep suspicion. If a car can be proved to have been rebuilt on a new Lotus frame, it is obviously far more valuable than one with a botched-up chassis.

Although I have already covered this in the chapter on the Elan, perhaps I should once again emphasize the importance of assembling the hubs on the proper sides, when cars have centre-locking wheels. The rule is RIGHT-HAND threads on RIGHT-HAND side, LEFT-HAND threads on LEFT-HAND side, and the wheel will come off if you get it wrong.

Spare parts do not usually present much of a problem. Many of them are common to popular cars, such as the Triumph Spitfire and Vitesse, and it is Lotus policy to look after the owners of their models which are no longer current. Elan gearbox parts come from Ford, which ensures their quality as well as their availability; the same goes for the Renault transmission of the Europa.

As for the engine, the twin-cam is a sturdy unit, and provided that it has something like 40 psi oil pressure above 3,000 rpm it should go on for years of ordinary road use. If it's smoky, of course, it may be in need of a rebore, but a moderate consumption of oil is normal — I would be worried if it didn't use any! It rarely remains clean for long, indeed it is difficult to avoid a few slight oil leaks, which are not detrimental. A little oil around the engine is a good thing, as it keeps the front end of the chassis from rusting; the same applies to the final-drive, which usually leaks a bit and preserves the rear of the frame.

The most important thing to check is the long timing chain, and if the bolt that adjusts it is almost screwed home — beware! If the chain actually rattles, don't run the engine any more until you have fitted a new one. This roller chain is not a weak point,

The great advantage of Elan or Europa restoration is that even if you find one with a badly or distorted body you can always replace it with a brand new shell, a supply of which are produced on the proper jigs by Lotus from time to time.

Total restoration is encouraged by the simplicity of the Elan backbone chassis and the accessibility which it affords to all the mechanical components, but you will have your work cut out to match the presentation of this Series 3.

but if it were ever to break all the valves would be scrap, probably all the pistons as well, and even the camshafts might be damaged. So, when in doubt, fit a new chain.

Perhaps I may be forgiven for remarking that extreme care should be taken in fitting the chain. It is terribly easy, by turning the crankshaft or one of the camshafts, to bring a valve and piston into contact, and valves can be bent so easily. Personally, I prefer to remove the head and set the camshafts on the bench, also setting the crankshaft while the head is off. Then replace the head, and fit the chain *without moving anything*. There are plenty of other methods, of course, but think twice, and then think again, at every step of the job. Even experienced mechanics have bent valves by doing this assembly in a hurry, and if the timing isn't right, the valves are likely to come in contact with the pistons when the engine is first turned over.

Any work on the distributor means taking off the carburettors and don't forget that the O-rings are there to prevent transmission of vibration, so these instruments must be loosely mounted. A lot of end float on the water pump spindle indicates that replacement time is near. Before buying an Elan, it is advisable to take a long enough run to make sure that overheating is not a problem. The cooling always tended to be somewhat marginal and it may become inadequate for some simple reason, such as failure to replace the plates or packing that direct the airflow into the film block.

As the Lotus factory is now fully occupied with the current 2-litre engine, Ian Walker has taken over the twin-cam and is now the official reconditioner at Ian Walker Racing, 236 Woodhouse Road, London, N12. All the necessary spare parts are being manufactured and Ian can rebuild any twin-cam engine, irrespective of what sort of nick it's in. So, there is simply no possibility of this engine becoming an orphan.

Ian is a great Lotus enthusiast and raced these cars for many years. Indeed, all the Lotus dealers that I have come across appear to be red hot enthusiasts for the *marque*, which seems a good reason for going Lotus when choosing a classic sports car to cherish.

As to which Lotus to buy, that is quite a problem. For the man who must have a mid-engined car, the Europa chooses itself. The Europa Special, with twin-cam engine and five-speed gearbox, is obviously the ultimate, but they are very pricey. On the other hand, the less glamorous S2 (not S1!), with Renault engine, is in far less demand and may well be a bargain for the impecunious. It's rather like a certain well-known motorcycle tuner who, when asked how fast he could make a stated bike go, always replied, ' 'Ow much money 'ave yer got?'

The +2 is for many the ideal Lotus. There is enough space for it to be used as a practical, everyday car, especially when children or dogs are often carried. Some consider that it's the best-handling Lotus of all, and the last ones made had a high fifth gear for quiet, economical cruising.

As for the Elan, there's nothing quite like it for putting enjoyment back into motoring. Its small size is such an advantage in traffic and its fuel economy makes a lot of sense nowadays. As to which Elan to buy, again it's a question of money. The cars improved all the time, right up to the big-valve Sprint, which was the daddy of them all.

However, many of the earlier cars have been brought up to date by enthusiastic owners through the years. For example, it's unlikely that there are any Elans still running around without sleeves for the valve buckets that previously slid directly in the aluminium, while the soft rubber doughnuts, that wound up and unwound, have mostly been replaced by reinforced ones.

To modify a Lotus is to reduce its market value, but to improve it in accordance with the later specification, or to fit the Special Equipment options, is to make it a more desirable car. So many manufacturers spoil their cars when they 'improve' them, and one therefore prefers their earlier models, but when Colin Chapman alters his designs, it's always for the better.

The Lotus twin-cam engine, clutch and gearbox assembly ready for installation. Even if you do not go so far as a complete strip-down and inspection it is advisable to take a close look at the long timing chain and its adjustment bolt. If there is any sign of stretch, replace the chain and save yourself a lot of money.

APPENDIX A

Technical specifications and performance data — Lotus Elan

S1 1962, S2 1964, S3 1965, S4 1968, Sprint 1971

Engine: (October 1962 to May 1963) 4 cylinders 81.5 × 72.75 mm (1498 cc) 100 bhp. 22 built, all replaced by 1558 cc units. (May 1963 to August 1973) 4 cylinders 82.55 × 72.75 mm (1558 cc). Standard 105 bhp @ 5,500 rpm, Special Equipment 115 bhp @ 6,000 rpm, Sprint 126 bhp @ 6,500 rpm. Compression ratio 9.5:1, Sprint 10.3:1. Cast-iron cylinder-block, 5 main bearings. Aluminium-alloy cylinder-head, inclined valves at 27° to the vertical, operated by twin, chain-driven overhead camshafts. Valve diameters: inlet 38.760/38.862 mm, Sprint 39.624/39.776 mm, exhaust 33.553/33.655 mm. Dual valve springs.

Valve Timing	Standard	S/E and Sprint
Inlet opens	22° BTDC	26° BTDC
Inlet closes	62° ABDC	66° ABDC
Exhaust opens	62° BBDC	66° BBDC
Exhaust closes	22° ATDC	26° ATDC

Cast-iron crankshaft, steel with nitralloy-hardened journals for competition engines, main journals 53.987/54.000 mm, crankpins 49.199/49.211 mm diameter. Steel-backed lead-bronze main and big-end bearings with lead overlay. Forged H-section steel connecting rods. Solid-skirt tin-plated aluminium-alloy pistons with 2 compression and 1 oil control ring. Floating gudgeon pins retained by circlips. Eccentric-lobe oil pump, 35–40 psi pressure, full-flow filter, driven by skew gear on jackshaft. Distributor driven by same gear.

Ignition timing

Weber carburettors ('A' pistons)	12° BTDC
Weber carburettors ('C' pistons)	10° BTDC
Weber carburettors (Sprint)	12° BTDC
Zenith-Stromberg carburettors	9° BTDC
Zenith-Stromberg (exhaust emission)	5° BTDC

Sparking plugs Champion N7Y with 0.020/0.023 in gap. Autolite AF32 with 0.025 in gap for exhaust-emission engines, except for sustained high-speed Champion N7Y.

Fuel pump driven by eccentric on jackshaft, drawing petrol from 9¼-gallon rear tank.

Carburettors: 2 twin-choke Webers, 40 DCOE 18 or 40 DCOE 31; or 2 twin-choke Dellortos, DHLA 40, or 2 constant-vacuum Zenith-Strombergs, 175 CD 2S, or 175 CD 2SE for exhaust-emission engines (Zenith-Strombergs only used in UK from November 1968 to August 1969).

Transmission: Borg and Beck 8 in diaphragm-spring clutch with hydraulic operation. 4-speed synchromesh gearbox with central lever, ratios:

	Semi-close	Close-ratio
Top	1.000	1.000
3rd	1.395	1.230
2nd	2.009	1.635
1st	2.971	2.510

Chassis-mounted hypoid final-drive, ratio 3.90:1 (S1, 2, and early 3), 3.777:1 (later S3 onwards), or 3.555:1 (optical). Drive-shafts to rear hubs with Rotoflex universal-joints.

Chassis: Central box-section backbone with fork extensions at each end and cross-members at their extremities, carrying saddle-mounted glass-fibre body. Engine and gearbox mounted in front fork, with propeller shaft through centre of backbone and final-drive at rear.

Independent front suspension by wishbones, coil springs and telescopic dampers, with anti-roll bar. Rack-and-pinion steering. Strut-type independent rear suspension with built-in telescopic dampers, coil springs, and tubular bottom wishbones. Girling hydraulic disc brakes on all four wheels, servo on S/E and Sprint models. Steel wheels, bolt-on standard but knock-on optional from S2 onwards.

Tyres: S1 had 5.20-13, later 145-13, S4 (March 1968) had flared wheel arches and 155-13 was S/E option, finally 155 HR 13 was standard.

Equipment: 12-volt lighting and starting, with DC dynamo. Speedometer, rev-counter, oil-pressure, water-temperature and fuel gauges. Heating, demisting and ventilation system. Electrical window operation (from S3, September 1965). Windscreen wipers and washers. Flashing direction indicators. Retractable headlamps.

Dimensions: Wheelbase 7 ft 0 in. Track (front) 3 ft 11 in, (rear) 4 ft 0 in. Overall length 12 ft 1 in. Width 4 ft 8 in. Weight 14 cwt.

Performance: Maximum speed of early models with 3.90:1 hypoid 108 mph with rev-limiter, 114 or 115 mph without. Sprint with 3.55:1 hypoid, 121 mph with rev-limiter, 124 mph without.

Acceleration 0–60 mph, 1964 8.7s, 1967 7.6s, 1970 7.3s, 1971 Sprint 6.7s.

Fuel consumption: 26 to 30 mpg.

Price:

Component form		Complete, with purchase tax
1964	£1,187	£1,436
1970	£1,595	£2,084
1971 Sprint	£1,663	N/A

APPENDIX B

Technical specifications and performance data — Lotus Plus 2

+2 1967, +2S 1968, +2S 130 1971, +2S 130/5 1972

Engine: 4 cylinders 82.55 × 72.75 mm (1558 cc). 118 bhp @ 6,250 rpm. Compression ratio 9.5:1. +2S 130 Feb 1971, 126 bhp @ 6,500 rpm. Compression ratio 10.3:1. Twin chain-driven overhead cam-shafts. 2 Weber 40 DCOE carburettors, twin Zenith-Strombergs on exhaust emission engines only. 13-gallon fuel tank. Other details as for Elan.

Transmission: Borg and Beck 8 in diaphragm spring clutch with hydraulic operation. 4-speed synchromesh gearbox with central lever, 5-speed on +2S 130/5, ratios:

	4-speed	5-speed
Overdrive	—	0.80
Top	1.000	1.00
3rd	1.395	1.37
2nd	2.009	2.00
1st	2.971	3.20

Hypoid final-drive, ratio 3.77:1. Drive-shafts to rear hubs with Roto-flex universal-joints.

Chassis: Central box-section steel backbone with saddle-mounted glass-fibre body. Independent front suspension by wishbones, coil springs and telescopic dampers, with anti-roll bar. Rack-and-pinion steering. Strut-type independent rear suspension incorporating spring-damper units, with tubular bottom wishbones. Servo-assisted disc brakes. Knock-on steel wheels, fitted 165-13 tyres. Other details as for Elan.

Equipment: 12-volt lighting and starting with DC dynamo, alternator from +2S onwards. Speedometer, rev-counter, ammeter, oil-pressure, water-temperature and fuel gauges. Voltmeter and clock on +2S 130. Heating, demisting and ventilation system. Electrically-operated windows. 2-speed windscreen wipers and washers. Flashing direction indicators. Retractable headlamps.

Dimensions: Wheelbase 8 ft 0 in. Track (front) 4 ft 6 in, (rear) 4 ft 7 in. Overall length 14 ft 0 in. Width 5 ft 3.5 in. Weight: +2 16.8 cwt, +2S 130/5 17.5 cwt.

Performance: Maximum speed 121 mph (mean), 125 mph (best one way). Acceleration 0-60 mph: +2 8.2s, +2S 7.7s, +2S 130 7.4s.

Fuel Consumption: 25 to 28 mpg.

Price:

Component form		Complete, with purchase tax
1967 +2	£1,672	£1,923
1971 +2S 130	N/A	£2,626
1972 +2S 130/5	N/A	£2,826

Technical specifications and performance data — Lotus Europa

S1 1966, S2 1969, Twin-Cam 1971, Europa Special 1972

Engine: Renault 4 cylinders 76 × 81 mm (1470 cc) 82 bhp @ 6,000 rpm. Federal emission engine 77 × 84 mm (1565 cc) 80 bhp @ 6,000 rpm. Compression ratio, both versions, 10.25:1. Die-cast aluminium cylinder-block and head, 5 main bearings, cast-iron liners, pushrod-operated overhead valves. Twin-choke downdraught Solex carburettor, mechanical fuel pump, 7-gallon tank.

Twin-Cam 4 cylinders 82.55 × 72.75 mm (1558 cc) 105 bhp @ 5,500 rpm, compression ratio 9.5:1.

Europa Special 126 bhp at 6,500 rpm, compression ratio 10.3:1. 2 fuel tanks containing 12½ gallons with twin-cam engine. Other details as for Elan.

Transmission: Single-dry plate clutch with cable operation. 4-speed synchromesh gearbox with central remote control, 5-speed gearbox on Europa Special only, ratios:

	4-speed	5-speed
Overdrive	—	0.87
Top	1.03	1.21
3rd	1.48	1.60
2nd	2.26	2.33
1st	3.61	3.62

Hypoid final-drive, ratio 3.56:1, 5-speed 3.77:1. Drive-shafts to rear hubs with Hooke's universal-joints.

Chassis: Central box-section steel backbone with fork extension at rear, carrying saddle-mounted glass-fibre body. Engine, gearbox and final-drive mounted in one unit within rear fork. Independent front suspension by wishbones, coil springs and telescopic dampers, with anti-roll bar. Rack-and-pinion steering. Independent rear suspension by trailing radius-arms and upper and lower links, fixed-length drive-shafts forming upper links, with coil springs and telescopic dampers. Disc front and drum rear brakes, servo standard with twin-cam engine, extra on S1, S2. Bolt-on steel wheels, fitted 155-13 tyres; extra, light-alloy wheels fitted 175/70-13 front and 185/70-13 rear tyres.

Equipment: 12-volt lighting and starting with alternator. Speedometer, rev-counter, ammeter, oil-pressure, water-temperature and fuel gauges. Heating, demisting and ventilation system. Electrically operated windows from S2 onwards. 2-speed windscreen wipers and washers. Flashing direction indicators.

Dimensions: Wheelbase 7 ft 8 in. Track (front) 4 ft 5.5 in, (rear) 4 ft 5 in. Overall length 13 ft 1.5 in. Width 5 ft 4.5 in. Weight: S2 13.1 cwt, Special 14.0 cwt.

Performance: Maximum speed: S2 109 mph (mean) 115 mph (best), Twin-Cam 117 mph (mean) 120 mph (best), Special 121 mph (mean) 123 mph (best). Acceleration 0–60 mph: S2 9.5–10.7s, Twin-Cam 7.0–8.2s, Special 6.6–7.7s.

Fuel consumption: 26 to 30 mpg.

Price:

Component form		Complete with purchase tax
1969 S2	£1,275	£1,667
1971 S2	£1,459	£1,918
1972 Twin-Cam	£1,595	£1,995
1973 Special	£2,044	£2,471

Extra: Brand Lotus light-alloy wheels and Firestone tyres £101.

Technical specifications — Lotus 47

47 1966–7, 47A 1968

Engine: Mark 13C Lotus Cosworth, 4 cylinders 83.5 × 72.75 mm (1594 cc). 165 bhp @ 7,000 rpm. Compression ratio 11:1. Twin chain-driven overhead camshafts. Tecalemit-Jackson fuel-injection, replaced by two twin-choke Weber DCOE 45 carburettors on most non-works cars. Electric fuel pump, 2 fuel tanks containing 20 gallons. Dry-sump lubrication.

Transmission: Borg and Beck $7\frac{1}{2}$ in clutch with hydraulic operation. Hewland FT 200 5-speed gearbox with remote control, in unit with differential. Drive-shafts to rear hubs with outer Hooke's and inner Rotoflex doughnut joints.

Chassis: Central box-section steel backbone with fork extension at rear, carrying saddle-mounted glass-fibre body. Engine, gearbox and final-drive mounted in one unit within rear fork, with hoop-shaped rear cross-member embracing transmission housing. Independent front suspension by wishbones, coil springs and telescopic dampers, with anti-roll bar. Rack-and-pinion steering. Independent rear suspension with light-alloy uprights, upper tubular links, reversed lower wishbones, and long tubular upper and lower trailing arms, with anti-roll bar. Dual-circuit disc brakes with twin master-cylinders and balance bar. Centre-locking, peg-drive magnesium-alloy wheels, 7.5 in front, 10 in rear rims, with three-eared spinners, fitted 550 × 810 × 13 front and 600 × 1050 × 13 rear tyres (original sizes).

Equipment: 12-volt lighting and starting with alternator. Speedometer, rev-counter, ammeter, oil-pressure, oil-temperature and water-temperature gauges. Face-level vents. Windscreen wiper. Flashing direction indicators.

Dimensions: Wheelbase 7 ft 7 in. Track (front) 4 ft 5 in, (rear) 4 ft 0 in. Overall length 13 ft 1.5 in. Width 5 ft 4 in. Height 3 ft 4 in. Ground clearance 3.75 in. Weight 10 cwt 10 lb. Weight distribution with fuel, oil and driver 45% front, 55% rear.

APPENDIX E

Lotus Elan and Plus 2 chassis identification

Date	Chassis number		Date	Chassis number	
January 1963	26/0001	Elan 1500 introduced	March 1968	45/7895	Series 4 convertible introduced
May 1963	26/0026	Hardtop optional		36/7896	Series 4 fhc introduced
January 1964	26/0330	Model continued	November 1968	50/1280	Stromberg carburettors on +2 fhc
November 1964	26/3901	Series 2 introduced			
January 1965	26/4325	Series 2 continued		45/8600	Stromberg carburettors on Series 4
September 1965	36/4510	Series 3 fixed-head coupé introduced			
			March 1969	50/1554	+2S fhc introduced
November 1965	36/5147	Close-ratio gearbox available	August 1969	45/9524	Weber carburettors reintroduced on Series 4
January 1966	26/5207	Convertible continued			
	36/5201	Fhc continued	December 1969	50/2407	Final +2 fhc
	26/5282	Special Equipment convertible available		50/2536	Final old numbering of +2S fhc
				45/9823	Final old numbering of Series 4 convertible
June 1966	26/5810	Final Series 2 convertible			
	26/5798	Final Series 2 Special Equipment convertible		36/9824	Final old numbering of Series 4 fhc
	45/5702	Series 3 convertible introduced	January 1970	7001 010001	New chassis-numbering system with suffix to identify models: A=S4 fhc; C=S4 convertible; E=S4 S/E fhc; G=S4 S/E convertible; L=+2S fhc
	45/5701	Series 3 Special Equipment convertible introduced			
July 1966	36/5977	Series 3 Special Equipment fhc introduced			
January 1967	45/6678	Series 3 convertible continued	February 1971	7101	Elan Sprint fhc and convertible and +2S 130 introduced
	45/6680	Series 3 Special Equipment convertible continued	January 1972	7201	Models continued unchanged
	36/6679	Series 3 fhc continued	October 1972	7201	5-speed gearbox optional on +2S 130
	36/6683	Series 3 Special Equipment fhc continued			
June 1967	50/0001	Plus 2 fhc introduced	January 1973	7301	Models continued unchanged
August 1967	45/7328	Series 3 convertible continued	August 1973	7301	Elan Sprint fhc and convertible discontinued
	45/7329	Series 3 Special Equipment convertible continued			
	36/7327	Series 3 fhc continued	January 1974	7401	+2S 130 and +2S 130/5 continued but gradually phased-out over next year
	36/7331	Series 3 Special Equipment fhc continued			